The Road to Ascension

A Telepathic Transmission
from the Arcturian Collective

Channeled through Jan Mahloch

Library of Congress Cataloging-in-Publication
Mahloch, Jan
The Road to Ascension
A Telepathic Transmission from the Arcturian
Collective channeled by Jan Mahloch
ISBN #978-0-578-83025-4

Trio3 Press

Dedication

To Mary, Katlin and Sandy who have nurtured and
encouraged my channeling ability.

To my husband, son and daughter-in-law for their
unconditional support and love.

To all the clients who have trusted me with their light.

A Note from Jan

This book is the result of my three-year awareness of and communication with the Arcturian light beings. Their first contact with me was through the use of symbols. I found myself waking up in the middle of the night and drawing unrecognizable symbol-like images. It was through these images I became sensitive to the Arcturian energy and was consequently able to write their messages. The more I spent time in connecting to their energy of light, the easier it was to telepathically connect. Their vibration is quite different from the vibration of the angelic realm to which I was accustomed. I had spent many years channeling messages for clients from Archangel Michael and have to admit I was reluctant to move on from what was familiar to me. With the encouragement of the angels and close friends, I made the leap by walking my own road to ascension, accepting myself as a channel for multi-dimensional guides. Working with the various dimensional light energies is a rewarding experience and I am grateful for the guidance that has been given to me along the way. It is clear to me that the ascension process is for everyone and that the support for this journey is here. Validation for this comes from the fact that I am an ordinary person living what many would call a normal life. I worked for years as a registered nurse and raised a family, all the while seeking my spiritual purpose. I feel that the discoveries of my own ascension journey have barely begun but I am confident the Arcturians and many other light beings are here to help us unlock our own innate wisdom. Channeling this book was a privilege and I hope it serves your journey.

Jan

Introduction

We are the Arcturians. We are a collective of multi-dimensional light. We have transcended the ascension phase in which you currently find yourself. We are a stable energy of many. For eons we have moved through the many phases of multi-dimensional light to the expression of what we are today in your real time. We are not human nor have we ever been. Our world is quite different from yours but similar in that we are all citizens of the vast universe. We are charged with the education and awareness of this fact. You are to realize that you are much more than you can conceive yourself to be. As far as your place in the universe, you are an unrealized potential at this point in your time. We are here to assist you in developing that potential to further your own evolution. Your potential comes with choices to be made, blinders to be removed and concepts to contemplate. This is the goal of this book. We will always present, as the collective we are, these concepts for your education of universal law and truths.

In this book we will not spend time telling you about our existence because what is important now is your existence as the humanity that is living on an ascending planet. Our journey has been different and sharing the details of our evolution will not be helpful to you. What will be helpful to you is for us to focus on your evolution providing the details, methods and knowledge that you need to seamlessly make this adjustment into your new world. We are also ever watchful of the energies of planet earth and how they influence the speed of the ascension journey. Time is not a concept we concern ourselves with, although, we are aware of its importance on life on your planet and will be mindful of this when suggesting procedures.

We come to you as a collective of energy taking the form of many points of light. By presenting ourselves as a collective we can merge into one voice and demonstrate the strength of unity consciousness. Many of us can work in the forefront as multi-dimensional guides, however, we will always retain our connection to our collective. Due to our existence in unity consciousness, we know not the struggle of your ego or your individual pursuit to be separate from all that is around you. The great fallacy you live by is that you are separate, denying a universe teeming with life, holding the belief that you are unworthy of your connection to all that is and most of all your separation from each other and the earth. Your greatest hurdle is to recognize your original spark of light that is shared by dimensions of beings that await your return to this truth. The earth knows these truths and is the keeper of wisdom that has been ignored and shoved aside in your quest for individual pursuits. At the same time, the earth has had to hold a platform for humanity's collective consciousness that also consists of the distorted energy of the many who dwell within it. The earth has constantly shined the light of the ultimate unity consciousness as it keeps together the ebb and flow of a myriad of consciousness from the various kingdoms. It is the ultimate balance for the mineral kingdom, the animals, the elements and all of humanity. All of these energies are constantly at play and the earth is the hand that holds forth their existence as part of the universe. The earth knows its place in the universe, knows itself as a collective voice and consciousness. Its growing pains for its potential are surging forth as it becomes something quite extraordinary. Earth as a conscious voice is speaking to each and every one of you. Do you heed the call? Do you awaken from your unconscious slumber? This is your challenge to follow the example of the earth that you reside on and live your potential; live as a voice of unity all the while staying in integrity for the unique gift that you are.

If you are reading this book, you have been seeking something outside of your human existence in different stages of your life. Many call this seeking a spiritual path or the awakening of their consciousness. This journey has been fulfilling at times, frustrating at other times. What you have been seeking has been a part of you all this time but the full realization of this fact has eluded you. The frustration comes from the knowing that truth is there but try as you might you cannot reach it and anchor it into your reality. You may be aware of certain universal truths but their expression into your world is elusive. You constantly look outside yourself for this validation and this is your default mode. No matter the experience you may have beyond the 5 senses you look to your world for the validation of that knowing. "Prove it," is your mantra.

The proof you are looking for comes primarily from your own experience and applying the energy of light to all you create. This experience comes from knowing your multi-dimensional self as the light that you are. It comes from the awareness of your connection to unity consciousness and to an ascending planet. And finally, it comes from untethering from a collective consciousness that neither supports your light nor validates your experiences with your dimensional self. Striving for that awareness, experiencing your light and releasing that which holds you back is what we call the ascension process. We will present key concepts that will help you understand, stabilize and utilize the energetic changes that are vital to this process. The ascension process is an integral part of humanity's evolution and our information can assist in this global shift. The centerpiece of this process is the energy of light and the discovery of that potential through your multi-dimensional self. This part of your beingness has barely been explored and the intention to do so will send you on a path of purpose and creation humanity has never known. Learning to experience and care for this integral energy of light is necessary and rewarding. We are charged with giving you the information to help you know this energy and subsequently become a creator from it. Managing your light within the human experience is critical to your balance and success. Your success with the ascension process comes from the realization that you are and have been tied to a collective consciousness that no longer supports or assists you in reaching the purity of your connection to all that is. In our review of this consciousness, we will show you how it holds you back from fulfilling your earthly purpose and experiencing the joy that is your birthright. The untethering process from the collective consciousness becomes easier when you experience that which you truly are; a creator of the light. The actualization of this fact is happening simultaneously with your participation as your human-self living on a changing dimensional planet. Like you, the planet is expanding into the light that it knows itself to be but unlike you it has already chosen to participate in its own ascension process. You are at your most magnificent choice point. A choice point that beckons you to see yourself as more than human and more than just the consciousness with which you are comfortable. It beckons you to see yourself as the multi-dimensional light that you are. We, the Arcturian collective and citizens of the universe hope you will allow us to help you participate fully in the ascension process that lies ahead. And in so doing, you will receive the universal support that will assist you in knowing yourself as part of the unity consciousness that is alive and well in the new emerging world of planet earth.

We celebrate you for taking the time to ponder the following information and concepts. We celebrate you for choosing to participate in the ascension process and expressing the gift of your light. And most of all we celebrate your courage and strength to help humanity transform in this critical time of its evolution.

Table of Contents

Part 1

THE ROAD TO ASCENSION

The Collective Consciousness

At this present time your world is tethered to a vibration called the collective consciousness. Imagine a large cloud of energy that looms over your world tying each human to it by an energetic cord. This cloud contains all the beliefs, agreements and thought forms that were ever expressed by civilizations living on the earth. Collective consciousness began with universal truths but over time these truths have been overshadowed by human experiences both good and bad. Every culture has added to this energy by their own unique beliefs and expressions resulting in a heavy vibration that no longer serves humanity's evolution. The collective consciousness supports limitations, separation and extreme doubt in one's discovery of their light. It is at odds with your personal ascension path and it does not support a new dimensional earth. The earth has been purging itself of the energy of the collective consciousness because it has been anchored there by every human who has ever walked the earth. It is like a cloud that has been constantly overshadowing the earth skewing the light of universal truth. Over time this consciousness will change with the evolution and extreme healing of humanity. The ascension process and the awareness of the multi-dimensional self will usher in a transformation from collective consciousness to unity consciousness. The new vibrational earth supports unity consciousness and all who seek it. Until this time of transformation, working with the dimensional self assists you in disconnecting from the collective thoughts and beliefs that no longer serve you. The more time you spend with your light and communicating with universal truth the less you are influenced by the collective. You free yourself from the untruths that distort and mask your light. Many are detaching from the collective as they discover the wonders of their light and this erodes away the energy of the collective. It is a process of peeling back the myriad layers of this consciousness to once again shine a light on the universal truth that has always been there.

Beliefs

You would need a powerful computer to chronicle all the beliefs that have ever been anchored on your planet. Beliefs are simply energy but over time they take on a power of their own which overrides truth. Truth is hard to come by as it has been distorted with the myriad of beliefs that humanity holds dear. What is truth and what is an entrenched belief that has been agreed upon many times over? These agreements of what is truth which are beliefs in disguise have been reinforced cementing layers of energy that must be vanquished to discover your core of truth within. Your beliefs have shifted your energy creating webs of distortion that mask the light that you are. You see the doubt, the fear and the confusion but rarely do you see the truth of yourself. It can take lifetimes to dissect all the beliefs you hold true but one stands out as the most important. Do you believe that you deserve the light that you are? The truth is that it is your birthright to be a human container full of light with vast potential for creation on planet earth. This truth should be your all-consuming focus releasing all beliefs that do not serve this truth. In the beginning of your ascension journey, this truth may seem intangible and difficult to come to terms with compared to your own belief system. Doubts will surface and you will look to others to validate this truth. The proof, however, lies within you and it will reveal itself as you summon up the strength to go forward discovering your light. Connection to the multi-dimensional self will illuminate what is possible and the remembrance that it is there for everyone. It is not about being deserving of the light but accepting the truth that you are the light. This acceptance of what you truly are facilitates the integration of vast amounts of light that is available to each and every one of you. So, take the time if you must to study and uncover the beliefs you hold or speed up your evolutionary process by looking at this one belief. Ask yourself "do you truly deserve to be the light that you are?"

Validation

The Collective Consciousness has trained you to look for validation when embarking on anything new. Humanity values the opinions and beliefs of others which can result in a lack of confidence or frustration for those that seek to further their evolution. The beliefs of the collective consciousness can oppose your intrinsic intuition and clarity of purpose. One of the strongest beliefs it supports is a hierarchy notion that there is always someone who knows better than you. This belief can become an obstacle to overcome when beginning the ascension journey. However, when following the path to your light, you are the expert and through frequent contact with your multi-dimensional self you will come to realize this. Confidence will blossom and purpose will become clear as you activate and assimilate more universal light. Discernment is still necessary as you walk this ascension path because you will from time to time fall back into patterns of relying on old beliefs. The energy of these old beliefs comes from a hierarchal system designed to separate instead of unify. This energy therefore fosters the act of seeking others' approval which seeds more doubt into your energy field. It is not a satisfying experience to be in pursuit of validation because you enter into a false competition with others. There is no need to compete in the light, everyone has the opportunity to meet their light-filled source of origin. There is no race to the finish thus the timing of your evolution is up to you. When you exist in unity consciousness, you become aware that all roads lead you to where you are going. There is enough creative energy for everyone, there is no judgment of your progress or ultimately how you choose to evolve. Your intention to be your ultimate light will illuminate your path and will show you what is correct and valid for you. Reach for this truth next time you seek validation from another for this results in living the truth of unity consciousness.

Hierarchy

The Collective Consciousness supports and maintains a hierarchal system. Central to this system is the belief that "power over" is more worthy or deserving than "power to." Those that demonstrate this belief are raised upward in the top tiers of esteem and leadership. Your limitations come from trying to rise to the top tiers at all costs. The message is clear that someone or something is better than the other. Thus, humanity must stay in a state of judgment in order to survive in this hierarchal system. Your adaptation to this system comes at an early age by adopting a competitive mode of operation. In all facets of your life you are encouraged to compete and compare yourself to others as you climb this hierarchal ladder. Even in a spiritual way, you seek to follow those whom you deem more evolved than you. You doubt your own wisdom and give authority over to those chosen few you have christened as your guru or leader. But who is truly evolved, those who expound their wisdom allowing themselves to be put up on a pedestal or those who truly live their wisdom? Is the purpose to seek spiritual wisdom to move up a tier in the collective consciousness and to be judged as evolved or is it to live in a state of integrity balancing the power energy you possess? By seeking from the intention of your integrity, which is free from beliefs of the collective, you become a step closer to unity consciousness. This is a pivotal time for humanity where the door is now open and the energy is supportive of a new way of thinking and being. This new unity consciousness supports creating from both an individual and collaborative approach. This is not about everyone thinking and being the same using one voice instead it valuing each individual and their unique contribution in creating the new emerging world. In unity consciousness, there is no hierarchy because the leader or guru lives within each and every human. The expression of wisdom and light is available to everyone and there is still a choice to be made on how to experience that state of the ever-evolving human existence. The difference lies in using your creative energy for anchoring your light and wisdom to the planet in collaboration with building a world based on balanced power. Creations and experiences serve to uplift not oppress others in other words give "power to" instead of competing for power where the end result is someone must always lose. The emerging new dimensional earth is seeking that balance as it evolves and humanity must adapt to these changes. The old earth has been tainted by this hierarchal system that separates human consciousness from every single living consciousness that resides on the planet. One tree is judged to be better than another, one animal is more valuable than another therefore the wholeness you seek can never be attained when working from this system. The harmony and peace you aspire to is living in the creative collaborative approach that unity consciousness supports.

Judgment

The hierarchal system of the collective consciousness reinforces the need to judge yourself and others. You cannot compete with others if you are not evaluating their progress compared to yours. That is why try as you might, it seems impossible to give up the habits and patterns of judgment. The consciousness you find yourself in has locked humanity into this judgmental energy. Although it is not beneficial to others for you to be in judgment of them, it is especially detrimental to you when you surround yourself in this energy. It sows the seeds of doubt within you and blocks the clear path to your light. Breaking free from these patterns is not easy when holding tight to the thoughts and beliefs of the collective consciousness.

True freedom from this comes with spending more and more time with your multi-dimensional light. That is where the real progress will be made. Real progress will begin by the awareness of and expansion into your inner light. This contact with your multi-dimensional self will connect you to universal intelligence and greater wisdom. Over time the light will smooth and polish your energy to give you the clarity on how to best participate in unity consciousness. This participation in the new consciousness is key to releasing the need to judge or compare yourself to others. Humanity seeks peace and it will find it when it can step into the dimensional light that is available now. Peace and harmony are human aspirations that are alive with potential and creative ability. However, these aspirations have not been actualized on planet earth due to the bondage that comes from the hierarchal system. As long as humanity continues to align itself with the present collective consciousness, peace will remain a goal that cannot be attained. In contrast, unity consciousness offers the opportunity to reside in the energy of peace and facilitates the many unique creations that can pour forth. Judgment falls away when humanity seeks their peace by acknowledging the light and reaching for unity consciousness. In essence, the more you strive for your light and the connection to your dimensional self, the need to judge will slowly fall away. Your light will illuminate your cycle of judgment where you can see clearly where your patterns are ingrained. The light will focus you on new beliefs about yourself and others. Perceptions will come from a place of universal wisdom not humanity's tired and antiquated beliefs. Additionally, your inner dimensional light will gently nudge you forward until one day you find yourself living from the purity of unity consciousness. You can progress at light speed moving through the ascension process benefiting yourself and others. The final result; you no longer carry the energy of judgment. Judgment is also the mental construct of the human survival instinct that has evolved firmly into the consciousness of duality. Within the consciousness of duality, choices are either good or bad never neutral. There are no gray areas to judgment which is contrary to the intention of living in unity consciousness. The act of constantly living in the state of duality of (good vs bad) keeps you from your light. Furthermore, it creates an emotional attachment that can result in suffering. This attachment to a belief keeps you in a mental state far away from your dimensional self. Many of you are trying to rid yourself of the patterns or habits of judgment with varying success. First there comes the conscious awareness of the fact that you engage in assessing everything around you and that there are constant choices being made based on weighing whether something is good or bad. Next comes the realization that constantly flexing this ability to judge can cause pain and suffering for you and others. Over time by examining your beliefs and choices through the lens of judgment this pattern becomes weaker but not fully eradicated. You still must overcome the pull of the collective consciousness and the duality of life which is your current reality. Try as you might, judgment prevails. Therefore, the best way to rid yourself of the endless cycle of judgment is to assimilate more light through connection with your multi-dimensional self. Awareness and examination of your beliefs is the first step that leads you to your light. The light of you leads you to that neutral peaceful place within where you become more a part of unity consciousness not duality. It is by this communion with your own light that will eventually release you from the endless cycle and patterns of judgment. The light will erode over time the habitual comparisons of choice that do not serve you or bring you peace. As you step into creating simultaneously from both your human and dimensional self, there will be no need to engage in judgment. What is right for you will always be revealed by your light.

Comparison

The energy of comparison is alive and well on your planet. This energy stems from the beliefs of separation and lack. The need to compare yourself to another is not only compelling but a learned response. In the separation consciousness you exist in, you have forgotten the wholeness of light you truly are which perpetrates competition, comparison and individuality to a fault. There is no room for unity consciousness to exist when residing in the energy of comparison. This energy has dimmed your light and will continue to feed and reinforce beliefs that attract suffering. Additionally, comparison sows the seeds of victimization and turns on a cycle of energy that plays out pattern after pattern. However, once you begin to know yourself as your multi-dimensional light the need for comparison is naturally diminished. Separation is a human creation and unity is a dimensional creation. Increasing your light through familiarizing yourself with your dimensional self, interrupts the flow of comparison energy which enables the expression of unity consciousness that is buried deep within you. This is another good reason to acknowledge this light-filled dimensional self that coincides with your human existence. The possibilities to access light through the multi-dimensional self are endless. This part of you has been lying dormant waiting for you to experience the wholeness and light that you are. It is your key to the peace you seek through a new paradigm of unity that attracts joy and fulfillment. Allow yourself to live in this light once again riding the flow of unity where the beliefs of separation and lack cannot exist. See yourself as the individual human that co-exists with the unified wholeness of light that you are.

Fear

Your planet has to constantly balance two forces; one is fear and one is love. These two emotions are entwined in the human experience until they are forever tainted from their collective expressions. Fear was originally a survival emotion, an internal warning system that functioned in a balance with a myriad of other emotions. During this time of transition of the earth, it has become a continuous background emotion that signals constant alerts muddying the water of feelings. Even during the most joyous times, background fear is still there creating a slow stress to the physical body. As a result, fear has now become the human's guiding light and the catalyst for action. It is not a journey of truth instead it is the journey of the many degrees of fear. The collective consciousness holds a belief system of fear which adds to the individual's own innate fears. This interconnectedness adds to the load of fear you carry each and every day. In this time of ascension, the emotions of fear are cascading out of control which makes humanity focus on the emotion of love. The feelings of love and the emotions that result from love are a gift to humanity. The ability to raise the energetic vibration by a mere thought of joyful and happy emotions is paramount to the balance of the energetic state. Try as you might these thoughts do not pack the power they once did due to the low level of the ongoing fear you carry. Love has become conditional and diminished by the collective consciousness. Joyful emotions are fleeting and do not have a lasting effect on the body. Once what was a perfect gift to humanity has now become an ideal that will never be reached. Seeking love at this time is fruitless for the ideal cannot be attained through the human experience. It is clouded with the fear of loss, guilt, grief and disappointment. However, the purity of love resides in the light and the multi-dimensional self where it can be re-born in a new world. These are the emotions of love that you seek but to find the purity once again you must open to the light of your multi-dimensional self. In the past, you found your connection to love by traveling through the heart space. Going forward you must connect to the solar plexus and the heart space for direct access to your dimensional light. The heart space must be connected to the solar plexus for the purity of love to be re-anchored to your consciousness and to the world around you. Then you can be that anchor that seeds the collective consciousness with the purity and clarity of love. Thus, expanding the emotions of joy, happiness and laughter without the ties to the energy of fear.

Neutrality

The collective consciousness holds the belief that feeling neutral about a given situation or an experience with another is a demonstration of apathy or non-caring. Nothing can be further from the truth. You have been conditioned to weigh in on issues and judgments that do not concern you and deplete your energy reserves. Seeking your multi-dimensional light assists you in using your energy wisely. When connecting to your true light, much of the collective consciousness falls away and you begin to live from a new place of energy. Your wisdom is connected to a vast universal intelligence that is free of collective consciousness thinking and opens the door to viewing the world from a fresh new perspective. It facilitates the observer in you where you step back and view your world from a place of equal energy exchange. Of course, there are revelations along the way as you learn about what people and situations trigger your energy and keep you from the observer state. These emotional triggers are a valuable tool for looking deep within and releasing old conscious patterning. Much of what keeps you from entering into a neutral state is your energy habits. Your energy activates from the trigger and runs a default mode of patterns. The energy of this is so strong there isn't time to seek a neutral state as an observer because the energy pattern drives your reaction. The consequence of this is far from the neutral state you so desire.

Neutrality is a true gift to another because it is the energy of accepting their light. Neutral energy cuts through the judgment and sparks authentic connection. You look at another from the lens of your light not through the lens of the collective consciousness that has conditioned you. Noticing their light opens up possibilities for personal growth and situational solutions. Neutral energy also paves the way for more positive emotions like joy, accomplishment and contentment. But why not strive for living in positive emotions instead neutral energy you may ask? At this time, you are still strongly connected to the collective consciousness, these positive emotions you feel can be mired in learned conditional energy that is tainted from years of expectations and unfulfilled desires. So, the joy you seek becomes fleeting because it originates from thought forms attached to the collective consciousness energy field. The benefit of striving to live in a state of more neutral energy is it fosters experiencing much more lasting happiness and peace due to a new connection to your pure light. You return to a playful energy that leads to genuine emotions instead of emotions resulting from habitual patterns. The true feelings of positive emotions stay with you longer through your connection to your dimensional light and consequentially will increase your capacity for neutral energy. This neutral energy then becomes a place where you create more positive emotions and actions. Ultimately, seeking neutrality starts an energy cycle between you and your positive emotions that is honest, reliable and free from conditioned habits and old patterns of energy. You create a life from true light and experience the uniqueness of you. This is where your true autonomy lies as you live from the truth of you instead of the distortions of the collective.

In Conclusion

The collective consciousness is a creative vibration that planet earth has accepted and anchored for humanity's expression and evolution. The collective consciousness stands as proof that humanity is a creator of their perceived realities. As you look closely at what energies fuel your world and the beliefs that are passed down through generations, you not only see how you have learned to participate but how it has served the experiences of struggle and pain. The earth can no longer hold or support the vibration of collective consciousness. This energy is transforming as the planet dimensionally changes. Humanity is now experiencing the chaotic and confusing changes inherent in this transformation. Humanity must realize that separation, hierarchy, and limiting belief systems must come to an end for their next stage of evolution to be realized. Humanity must grow up and join the legions of universal intelligence that express their vast potential within a unity consciousness. The earth is now ready to support humanity's vast reservoirs of light through their connection to the multi-dimensional self. Once humanity truly reaches and expresses its light, truth and true cooperation will strip away the beliefs and distortions of old, paving the way for humanity to anchor the new energy of unity consciousness. Truth and the purity thereof will illuminate the earth and its inhabitants to once again become the bright star in the universe that it was always meant to be.

The Ascending Earth

The earth carries on with or without you. Although you are connected to the earth and its constant rotation, you have less a hold over it than you might think. Can you alter its landscape, yes of course, but can you make it die? That is a fallacy of fear. You can ruin the earth for your existence but you cannot truly destroy the earth. It has been here before you and it will be here when you leave. It has been transformed many times in its form and it will continue to take evolutionary form. The earth is not the constant you think it is, just as many planets in your solar system have changed form through eons of time. Again, you look to the earth's form in a linear time instead of looking at it as the dimensional form that it is and you are. Try communicating with the earth from your dimensional form and you will experience a different earth that only appears to you without the use of human senses. Your senses are showing you a distortion of the earth that is not its full potential. Much like you, there is more to the earth than meets the eye. To know the earth in all its potential and fascination, is to communicate with the earth dimensionally. This is where you get to know the planet you hold so sacred. You have yearned for such closeness with the earth for you have had these conversations and glimpses of possibilities in your dream state. You cannot be on this planet and not feel the deep connection you have for the earth. You have a connection to the earth like no other place in the universe. It has been the home of the human experience and has felt every evolutionary growing pain. It has been a playground of free will and choice, of struggle and loss, joy and celebration. It has been exploited many times over and still exists intact in a constant orbit of light. Just look at the crystal kingdom that the earth has offered its inhabitants. These crystals are the earth's light in useable form. Who cannot look at glittering faceted stone and not see the light? These stones hold and magnify the earth's light and maintain a constant flow of energy upon the earth just as you do. You are becoming aware of your dimensional trail of light and learning to activate its ultimate brightness. This light illuminates your progress on your ascension journey which enables your recognition of the new emerging earth. This new earth has a higher vibration and a dimensional depth that will seed the light of each and every human on the planet. It is a wonderous vibration of potential and creation that has not yet been realized. This new emerging earth will be the foundation of unity consciousness through the emission of pure light. It will no longer hold the familiar energetics of the past. Those that walk the ascension path are now seeding the earth with their light building the foundation of unity consciousness with each step they take. This in turn is the preparation needed for humanity to further wake up and live in harmony and peace within this new dimensional world. Your advancement in knowing your multi-dimensional light coincides with the transformation of earth into its new dimensional state. The earth's energetic journey is the support and energy you need to live and demonstrate unity consciousness. Additionally, the earth's new vibration and magnetics assists you in the necessary energetic changes of your mental, emotional and physical bodies. Together you progress with a myriad of opportunity and creative energy that shapes the future of planet earth and its inhabitants.

Echo

The ascending earth has been signaling to the universe through a vibration of distress. Many universal light beings are heeding this call and are ready to be of assistance in the ascension process. Up to this point the earth projected a different vibration and heard only the dull echo of universal light. As the earth moves dimensionally, it can now respond to a resonance of overwhelming light. This was not possible before humanity chose to participate in multi-dimensional light. Just the mere human awareness of this light has made it possible for the universe to echo back to the earth and support the earth in taking its place as a fuller expression of the universe. The distress call has been replaced with a call for wisdom through telepathic communication and human acknowledgement of their knowing of their dimensional self. This vibratory echo is growing and the potential of this energy is enormous for the actualization of the ascension process. Listening to this light-filled universal echo can speed the transformation of the ascension process. This echo grows as you reach out to it inviting it in to your body of awareness. The light you emit is a signal to the universal helpers that you are in alignment with this resonance, and therefore, all the necessary tools for expansion of your light will be provided. Use your intention to call forth that which you need to support your ability to bridge your multi-dimensional and human self.

Animals

The earth has been the support and foundation of a variety of consciousness that continues to evolve with the planet. Animals are one such consciousness and their purpose is one of service. Many animals have come here from other dimensions and some were actually created on earth. Both types of animal consciousness give specific service to the earth and the human existence. Animals originating from other dimensions have brought forth a telepathic intelligence and anchored it to the planet. They serve to inspire awe and wonder but most of all keep an energetic light balance for a changing earth. These animals are in service to the earth and communicate with the earth in a dimensional way. Many of these dimensional animals have left the planet, their service complete, leaving behind the mythology that is in ancient text. An example of a dimensional animal is the dolphin for it is highly intelligent, possesses its own telepathic language and when observed can inspire great wonder and joy. It waits for the time when the humans can commune with it in a telepathic dimensional way and learn the wisdom it carries. These animals anchor a necessary vibration which is a building block of ascension and dimensional potential. They carry the joy of light from their dimension of origin. They have committed to continue with an ascended earth and will survive the test of time. Another type of animal consciousness is the animals created specifically for the earth and the purpose of human existence. They have served as food, companions and protectors, balancing the animal life cycle. Now that the planet has ascended their roles are changing. Energetically some cannot remain on the earth in their present state. Vibrationally these animals must evolve consciously or perish. Does this mean you do not have to be concerned about extinction of animals? Yes and no, some will leave for their purpose is complete others will evolve with the awareness of the multi-dimensional human. There is deep intention from the connection between the human and the animals at this time. Those animals that are slated to dimensionally evolve on earth will be assisted by the human experience of returning to the multi-dimensional self. In time humans will know themselves as a consciousness that is connected to a web of consciousness like the animal kingdom. This knowing will assist the animals who chose to continue to serve the human and earth in light-filled balance.

The Mineral Kingdom

Another such consciousness the planet communicates with and relies on for light is the mineral kingdom. The earth is teeming with areas of rich crystals that can expand the magnetics and light to further its universal connection. Some areas of the planet have held portals of energy that work in harmony with these minerals paving the way for humanity's evolution. Specific highly charged areas are no longer functioning as the portals they once were. New portals of potential are opening and the purity of unity consciousness is being embedded by the dimensional shift of the planet. What once was a depository of minerals for humanity's use has now become a place of old energy ready for renewal. When working with the minerals, one must telepathically communicate with them and ask how one could be of service to these minerals. Like you these minerals have unrecognized potential and a consciousness that must transform to keep up with the ascending planet. They have a need to be liberated from old constructs in order to be perceived in new ways. Many of you have a strong connection to these minerals and your purpose to assist them will unfold as you walk your ascension path. Begin to communicate with these minerals from your multi-dimensional self, forging a rich and deep communication that lies in service. Their response may surprise you and at the very least awaken additional light within you. Partnering with the mineral kingdom assists the release of the old energies within the earth which supports planetary transformation.

The Purging Earth

There are many places on your planet that have been contaminated with the pain and struggle of humanity's energy. Repetitive patterns of violence and exploitation have created a cycle of energy that has lived buried within the earth. These territories of land are the demonstrations of how this energy continues to influence humanity's behaviors and beliefs. From generation to generation, the bond of conflict is furthered by the effects of past energies. Just as a pristine lake can be polluted by human activity so can the land be tainted by the struggles and battles stemming from the belief of separation. The collective consciousness supports the energy of extreme shifts in belief patterns and behaviors due to the underlying concept of separation. Humanity is entrenched in opposing energies that serve the few and not the whole. This energy has been seeded in the earth over eons of time as well as in the genetic fabric of the human existence. Now that the earth is finally purging this separation energy, humanity is triggered in an overwhelming way that leads to insurmountable conflict and resistance. This is a cycle of energy that the world is experiencing now as specific areas of the earth are shifting and transforming. This energy cycle begins by the earth awakening the genetic energy buried deep within humanity to respond by the energy of resistance. This resistance energy echoes back and forth, attracting more separation and judgment energy until balance cannot be maintained. Humanity then relives and plays out this resistance energy resulting in violence, struggle and pain; the keystones of separation. Therefore; the energetic purging of the earth is humanity's opportunity to purge itself of the energy of separation by disconnecting to the separation energy of the collective consciousness. The earth is ready to hold and support the seeding of new energy that embraces unity consciousness principles through the healing of resistance. Resistance energy is then replaced by adaptation, neutrality and transformational energies in the genetic codes of humanity by experiencing the light of the dimensional self.

Dystopia

At this juncture, the earth is purging the energies of bondage, injustice and authoritarian suffering that have been anchored by humanity's past memories, experiences and thought forms. An ascending earth can no longer hold this energy and must expel it in order to pave the way for unity consciousness. This expulsion can trigger an overwhelming fear of dystopia into the collective consciousness. The fear of a dystopian society is now once again a prominent theme that stems from the energy of separation. Dystopia is a thought form based in the fear of losing individuality or extreme separation from the light of all that it is. Although on the surface dystopia resembles total loss of autonomy and uniqueness of the human experience, in an energetic sense dystopia represents the loss of one's true wholeness. Therefore, this fear surfaces as humanity wakes to up to the fact that it is living in separation lacking its genuine connection to its energetic sovereignty. True freedom comes from connecting to your sovereignty that lives within your multi-dimensional self. Knowing your dimensional light and creating from it is the authentic expression of your individuality and uniqueness. In so doing, you live and experience your wholeness through the unity of universal light.

In Conclusion

The earth has been the cradle of humanity's great evolutionary experience. Once again it holds the promise and foundation of support that is necessary for the next step in your evolutionary process. The potential of its dimensional transformation is at the early stages of becoming actualized. These are exciting times for the earth as it once again plays the "Mother" role to a humanity that needs its guidance, nurturance and support on the journey of growing into a citizen of the universe. The planet is being held in a loving energetic embrace by a myriad of universal light beings that are ready to aid and serve this transformational time. The earth has said "Yes" to its dimensional self and is now asking you to do the same. The planet is standing by waiting for the creative expressions of unity consciousness that humanity can seed with their knowing of their light. Separation with its struggle and pain are no longer necessary components of an expanding consciousness that seeks its return to the light. The earth has cleared the way for humanity's next evolutionary step, one of knowing itself as light. Follow the ascension path the earth has set before you and walk with confidence experiencing the great potential of light that you are. Planet earth awaits and has become your most trusted dimensional partner in your next great evolutionary experience.

The Ascension Process

The ascension process that the earth is taking part in is already complete. It is not visible to you in your third dimensional time for the steps you see the earth taking is in linear time not universal time. Your multi-dimensional self can encounter this ascended planet when it fully knows itself. Thus, you must strive towards the melding and awareness of your multi-dimensional self with your human existence. You are constantly watching the reruns of yourself and all the existence that has played out on your planet. You cannot see the ascended planet before you while you are still tied to the past and to your individual creation of the future. When you create from lower vibrational dimensions you create a constant loop of what has been created again and again. In order to synchronize your awareness of this new ascended planet, you must act from the dimensional self, create from this place of full potential. Otherwise, you will repeat the past in a never-ending loop of human existence. Can you now see why it is important to get to know your multi-dimensional self? This is where the true evolution lies. You have a saying in your world "been there done that" and this is the truth of where you are now. You have played this 3rd dimension existence out. There is no more to be gained from living in this energy of one voice, one pursuit and the connection to an antiquated collective consciousness. It is time to free yourself from wearing the blinders of what has always been. These blinders keep you from seeing who you truly are. Potential is all around you because you carry it within you. You must mine it every day by communing with your dimensional self and allowing yourself to grow into the light that you are. In this process, you will be growing up. You have been existing as a child would on your planet but ascension is asking you to grow into the adult that is truly a citizen of the universe. Proof on the ascension journey comes from the knowing that the earth is supporting your quest into the multi-dimensional light. The earth is now holding a vibration that can ease your frustration and make it possible to experience that which you have always known. Its growth dimensionally can now become your dimensional growth. You have the foundation that planet earth is creating to truly walk your ascension journey. And like the earth you will know yourself as light. Additionally, continual proof and validation of this knowing begins with experiencing your light through the multi-dimensional self.

Experience the Light

When reaching for your light-filled evolution, having your own experience with your light is not only necessary but imperative. There is information that you need that only you can provide for yourself. To truly know your multi-dimensional light and this part of yourself you must experience it for yourself. It is not a mental process but a true experiential process. We are not saying information and guidance by others is not helpful but it is only the beginning of your ascension journey. You must spend the time connecting in whatever way makes sense to you to reach for the light and consequently become the light of your dimensional self. This knowing does not come from a step-by- step process of systems that have been developed by the collective consciousness. Those systems are hierarchal structures that serve separation and in some cases feed doubt. It is common when learning something new to take on doubt and most systems of teaching compound that energy. Leaving it up to you and your own private experience helps to release doubt and sets you on the path of being unshakeable. To truly live as both a multi-dimensional being and a human, you must be unshakeable in knowing 100% that you are light. Being unshakeable comes with experience and the resulting confidence that springs forth from being in your own light. There is no teacher better than yourself when embarking on the ascension path. Your inner wisdom is a wealth of guidance but it needs to be set free. Spending time with the intention of being in your light, exercising the light and feeling your light, unbinds the ties that keep you firmly entrenched in doubt and consequently keep you from seeking comfort from the opinions of others. Purposeful actions always spring forth from time spent going within the inner sanctum of your light. You know what is best for you and it can be revealed to you by light-filled actions. Your multi-dimensional self is a temple for contemplation, a library of guidance and an energetic battery of light, all waiting for a true connection to the human experience. You only need to explore this connection through intention and spending time in your own light. Seek out others who empower your exploration of self from an experiential process that fosters your personal and unique abilities. Information is only one part of the equation and is no substitute for your own familiarity and involvement in your inner light. Once again, we urge you to release the old systems of the collective consciousness that judge and direct you to one size fits all thinking. Trust your own inner light to guide you forward and in doing so you will receive the genuine validation that comes from knowing your light through the dimensional self. In other words, to trust fully in your inner light, you must illuminate it and experience it as one of your greatest resources. Relying on your 5 senses does not give you the opportunity to use this most valuable resource that which you call your imagination. It is through this ability to imagine and create in your mind's eye that true connection to all that you are becomes possible. However, this resource has been relegated to the belief that using imagination is childish and a time waster. Daydreaming is an example of this as many a teacher, parent or friend would call you back from such an activity. But what is daydreaming? It is a flow of energy you are familiar with that takes you to your creative visions. It is also your use of imagination and the ability to ponder and receive concepts. Daydreaming is a most natural way to channel and commune with the light and universal flow. It is an example of your early ability to receive telepathic information and tap into the dimensional self. It is a natural state of being that comes to you when you have briefly turned off the intellectual mind and allowed your energy to flow with the light. Daydreaming is telling yourself a story that is being written instantly by working with your imagination and creative flow. You muse and flow from one thought to the next releasing the need to see it materialize in 3-dimensional form. It may not have physical form but it is the ability to form thoughts, integrate knowing of yourself and open up to possibilities. In other words, be your own visionary. The more you allow your energy to flow this way, the more you remember your telepathic abilities.

Telepathy

The ascension journey will awaken parts of yourself that have been lying dormant until this time of light-filled evolution. Communicating with your light will come about in fascinating new ways. One such way is through telepathy. Telepathy is a gift to the human experience from the dimensional self. Layers upon layers of you exist dimensionally packaged in a physical form. These layers do not use your 5 senses, they use telepathy as the communication tool. The physical form uses 5 senses and the multi-dimensional self uses telepathy. As you remember and utilize your dimensional self, you strengthen your telepathic communication. Telepathy is the way of the universe as it is a flow of energy that bypasses physical form and senses. It is the knowing of a collection of vast wisdom that can travel at the speed of light. To become once again a citizen of the universe, you must use telepathy, the dimensional connection that resides deep within you. The concept of telepathy has been distorted in your world, marked with fear around the concept of knowing one's personal thoughts both good and bad. This belief has limited the exploration and use of this ability. It must be awakened and expanded within you to walk the ascension path. At this juncture, the goal is to communicate with your multi-dimensional self and those dimensional guides that can help you anchor universal wisdom to the human experience. To fully bridge your human self with your dimensional self, you must connect and receive from your telepathic ability.

Universal Intelligence

Part of the ascension process is once again connecting to and communicating with universal intelligence. In this process, you are aware of your light capabilities which is the hallmark of participating in a meaningful way as a citizen of the universe. It is all about the light and your quest to know your light-filled dimensional self. As you become reacquainted with this dimensional part of yourself, you begin to take the necessary steps to fulfill your destiny as a universal citizen. The blinders drop away and you reimagine a life where the earth is one important component along with many others in the vastness of dimensional space. The earth is no longer central; it is a collaborative partner with all the various life forms of an alive and awake universe. Your planet no longer becomes an experimental lab where it is observed but not taken seriously. As your consciousness explodes fully into ascension awareness, you guide humanity and your planet to take a meaningful part in the cosmic web of light. This is what you were always meant to do and you get there by acknowledging the truth that you are much more than your human existence; you are the light you seek.

Leveling Up

Your progress on the ascension path comes from communicating with your multi-dimensional light and spending time with those guides who reside in those dimensions. Whether it is through meditation, participating in energy events or having energy treatments, they all keep leveling up your vibration to a place where you become familiar with your own light. This familiarity is key to the expansion of your light and the retrieval of information through telepathy. As you level up, you begin to successfully create from your multi-dimensional light and release the tethers of collective consciousness. You no longer doubt your creations through measuring their outcomes by the old beliefs of the collective. Instead, you feel those synchronistic moments where all comes together for your benefit. Over time you receive the clarity you seek on the ascension path but it comes with exposing yourself to dimensional light. You must make the time to be in this energy. It does not have to have any specific purpose. In your world, you spend time with a close friend sometimes for an activity and other times as you like to call it "hanging out." Sometimes there is no agenda only the simple energy exchange of being close to each other's energy field which can be quite comforting. The same can be said for spending time in the light with no agenda and the knowing that this is also a place where you belong. You belong in your light, a place of comfort and illumination of your purpose on earth. This is where you experience the answers to age old questions like; why am I here, how do I evolve and how I am connected to the all? Additionally, your leveling up anchors extra light to the earth which is assistive to humanity and the various earth consciousness it supports. As you level up to a higher vibration you emit the light energy that the animals and plants need at this time to adjust to the rapidly changing earth. The light is never wasted. When you have had all you can assimilate, you give out the light to your environment. This may not be visible to you but this is the way the light works. So, the next time you have a few minutes of idle time, go within and "hang out" with your multi-dimensional guide feeling the light that is you. Each minute brings you closer to leveling up your vibration and bridging the gap between your human existence and your dimensional self.

In Conclusion

Embracing the ascension process, as the earth has, is humanity's next step in evolution. We cannot stress enough that you are ready for this powerful journey into your dimensional light. What may have been seen as out of reach is here waiting before you. Saying "Yes" to the abilities you possess that have been lying dormant until now will amaze and thrill you as you expand into your light. The ascension process asks you to realize and actualize your human existence from a place of dimensional light. This dimensional light can be found when you see yourself as a triad of energetic light. Through this simple geometric shape of a triangle, you can best understand how this part of yourself is waiting for your discovery. Imagine your physical container called the human being at one point at the base of a triangle. Your expanded consciousness of energy is represented by the second point at the base of the triangle. Finally, your multi-dimensional self is at the third point or the apex of the triangle. You are this triad of energy that is now ready to come together in unison to create and express purpose on the earth. You have known yourself as a human with conscious energy but now it is possible to add the familiarity and connection of the dimensional self through the light that you are. The ascension process is this journey to know yourself as this triad of energy and to recognize the abilities that pour forth from this communication of self. Part of this journey is the realization of your triad of energy and the other is the actualization of your creations based in pure dimensional light. Like many others in the universe, you will know yourself as the light potential you are and live each day of your existence from this place of light. You will no longer walk between worlds instead ascension asks you to build a bridge between what it means to be a human with consciousness and a dimensional being of light. Planet earth is now ready for your new creations that will be inspired by this bridge and the realization of knowing yourself as the pure origin of light that you are.

The Multi-Dimensional Self

The time has come to awaken that part of you that has a vast resource for connecting and communicating to universal light. You are a triad of pulsating energy, the base of which is made up of your physicality and what you may call your consciousness. At the apex of this energy triangle is your multi-dimensional self. This dimensional part of you has lain dormant in your awareness until planet earth could support the evolution of this truth. The multi-dimensional self is your capacity to communicate at will not only with a myriad of dimensional energies but to once again connect with the pure source of your light. This connection is where the purity of you exists. In other words, you are much more than a physical body having expanded moments of consciousness. Your dimensional self is the pristine energy of light that connects you to all that is and all that will ever be. Many of you have had knowing of this but the full

The Human Experience vs The Multi-Dimensional Self

Walking the earth as a human uses 5 senses or so you have been taught. You have not been taught how to remember any other way to experience your world. Many have accomplished perceiving the earth in an expanded way that does not limit them to their 5 senses. In fact, entire civilizations were built on that premise to experience the earth from both the dimensional side they carry and their 5 senses attached to a physical body. When you truly see yourself as much more than the physical container you reside in that is when you truly propel yourself along the ascension path. Once this awareness comes to fruition within you, it becomes exponential in nature. Exploding into the light of your potential and serving you in ways that you cannot imagine as a physical human. The human body is wonderous in many ways but it also has been designed to have limitations. You cannot hurl yourself over a cliff and take flight but your dimensional self can do just that. The dimensional self knows no limitations and can travel at will through space and time. Your civilization pursues a physical container for such traveling but the vehicle has always been with you. Using your energetic vibration of light, your imagination and strong intention can propel you places no rocket ship can go. The only limiting factor you face is your skepticism for concepts that cannot be proven by the 5 senses. Your skepticism is a barrier to your freedom and your potential. The energy of skepticism is entrenched in the collective consciousness to which you are tethered. As you go forward with new ideas, concepts and musing, something holds you back. That something is the belief, again deeply rooted in the collective consciousness, that thinking outside of the box will not be supported or will deem you abnormal. These are powerful beliefs that you fall back into that are running an unconscious stream of energy. At this juncture you must resist the idea that all must be proven with your 5 senses and that experiences you are having as you seek the light are valid. What holds you back from freely making it up as you go? At one point your entire world was made up by the creative thought of the human experience. Have you lost your ability to create in this way? Can you look now at yourself as a blank canvas and start to paint your life in a new way? This is the ultimate purpose you are charged with negotiating the old world of 5 senses with the new world of infinite possibilities yet to be created by you and put into form. Can you abandon all you know? Of course not; many have tried without success and that is not the goal of the ascension process. The journey of ascension is a school of learning on how to walk on both sides of the path, continuing to walk the path of human with 5 senses and walking the path of a dimensional being of light. This collaboration begins with the acceptance of the fact that you are a multi-dimensional being living within a human existence. It is not a choice of one or the other, it is the process of building a bridge between the two, existing and living from both. This becomes possible as you become more familiar with your multi-dimensional self. You have always known yourself as a human possessing the gift of emotions which provide the capability of experiencing various feelings. These human emotions should be seen as a special gift and the calling card of the human experience. However, at this juncture, you also possess the gift of knowing your own dimensional self and how it communicates to the light. The multi-dimensional self is your opportunity to begin to create from a vast potential of universal light. It opens the flood gates to a capacity of light that the physical human can over time assimilate and integrate for a unique expression of planet earth. This expression of light is rewarding beyond your wildest dreams.

The Physical Body

The physical body is a functional and amazing creation in the 3rd dimension. It was designed to operate on planet earth in the dimension you find yourself in as well as in the dimensional changes of the ascension process. However, it has its limitations and it evolves at a much slower speed than the potential of your multi-dimensional self.

These innate limitations were necessary when your consciousness was underdeveloped. Although the body has room to grow with an evolving consciousness, it remains a fragile container at best. Over time the multi-dimensional self will become stronger and the physical body will have to keep up. So how does the physical body keep up? The body must transform part of itself that directly communicates to the collective consciousness. For example, your neurological system and electrical impulses are swayed on a daily basis by the thoughts and inputs of others. Your own belief system has embedded many pathways that the brain runs on a default mode. Most of what you call your thinking brain is just a repository of old patterns that run on their own in a constant loop. Your brain is destined for much more development and will get there as your telepathic abilities increase. Your body must also release the vast storage of energies that hold you back from your multi-dimensional self. These energies are embedded deeply from repetitive patterns of emotions that do not vibrate with the light that you are. They signal to you through your receptors of pain, fatigue and muscular dysfunction. When these signals are ignored and the body can no longer store these energies it may result in illness and susceptibility to pathogens. It is crucial to feed the body light in increments all the while releasing these energies that block the light. The multi-dimensional self can expand rapidly but it is held back by the transformation of the physical body. You can work on both simultaneously, releasing the stored energy and becoming familiar with your dimensional self. Taking in vast quantities of light can help release the physical impediments but careful balancing and attention to the physical needs of the body is necessary. Light will stimulate the body to evolve with the ascension process but it takes the willingness to leave behind these old patterns so the light can actually be assimilated. The ascension process and the resulting partnering with the multi-dimensional self is a wonderous experience but one should not forget the development of the physical body. The dimensional self needs the physical body for full expression of the light's potential on planet earth. Hand in hand, each serves the other and the human experience becomes what it has always been destined for; to know it's light.

Body Language

Another one of your 5 senses that is important to your multi-dimensional development is through body sensations and their energetic transmission through physical movement. The body responds to changes in temperature, the vibration from auditory sounds, through touch and various visual stimuli. These adaptive measures have allowed humans to evolve and create safe environments. However, they are also the building blocks that can open up pathways to the multi-dimensional self. Universal truth can be validated by what some may call "full body chills." Intuitively your physicality knows truth and can receive signals from the dimensional self through pulsating feelings through parts of your body. The opposite is also true when you feel extreme fear or as you like to say "it makes my skin crawl." This first came about as an adaptive measure of survival but it is also the consequence of your physical unseen energy patterns.

Vibration

The human experience has a variety of vibratory energies depending on the emotional and mental state of the individual. Due to the stress energy that surrounds and permeates your planet at this time, staying in one balanced state can be challenging. Finding that balance is key to keeping your vibration in a neutral place which is optimum for keeping in coherence with your physicality. It is in the instability of vibration that becomes an attractive medium for illness and creating unwanted consequences. The vibration that serves your body is one where the energy is in harmony with both your multi-dimensional self and your physical body. The barometer for this vibration is the feeling of complete neutrality. It is not the emotional high and low or the mental high and low. Neutrality is the stillness you feel down deep in the center of your being that signals to you that all is well. It is a space where judgment is nonexistent. The pitfall one encounters, however, is the belief that neutrality is apathy or detachment from a situation or person. Nothing can be further from the truth. A neutral vibration is life-giving and opens the door for creative thought and actions. Additionally, it is the vibration of unity consciousness and where the true inner peace lives.

You are moving to a consciousness where the default is a neutral peaceful vibration that supports a stronger evolving physical body and a growing expanding dimensional self. There will be no need to ride a roller coaster full of unwanted vibrations. Seeking the neutral vibration is part of the ascension process and will become more evident as you progress. You will not need the highs and lows to signal to you that you are fully alive in a human existence. Stepping into your own maturity by carrying the neutral vibration of unity consciousness can illuminate another side to what you call humanity. The neutral vibration can show you how to actualize what you may have always dreamed of but never thought was possible.

Safety

Your human body has been wired with physiological mechanisms that help you survive your environment. These mechanisms are now out of balance due to the load of fear that all of you carry. It is not about actual physical survival but mental and emotional survival. All alerts have been awakened to the point that the human existence is walking a fine line to keep outward fear in check. Your human body was never intended to carry such a load of fear and survival energy. Thus, there is a breakdown of health and very few are immune to this breakdown or alteration in circuitry. Your brain has been rewired many times adding more and more survival beliefs that steer you in your everyday life. The world you see before you is but a mirage of these beliefs and the overwhelming survival mechanisms that the human race projects. The result is a false sense of safety built on a fearful existence and a constant tapping in to a fearful collective consciousness. Many techniques have been prescribed to feel emotionally safe, to go forward in a common-sense way but the result is limited. Until you can fully break free from the collective consciousness, safety will elude you. Breaking free is bridging the gap between your human existence and your multi-dimensional self. That is where the true peace lies as knowing yourself as the light that you are carries no human fear.

Energy Upgrades

As you seek the wholeness that is your birthright, you will discover your physical body will be changing with the light you assimilate. In the ascension process, your dimensional self continues to be activated to expand into the light which challenges the physical container that is you to upgrade itself. The light has to go somewhere flowing forward into the energy of the mental and emotional fields. This can cause disruption in those fields which may be blocked with old energy that is not in coherence with the new light of the multi-dimensional self. Many old patterns may appear coming out of the shadows to be transformed into the light of you. These old patterns need to be dissolved by a vibration upgrade and can cause physical symptoms such as fatigue, headaches, muscular pain and moodiness. You are challenging all of your energy fields with the assimilation of more light and the physical body must adapt. This adaptation is a process that will show you how fast you can integrate the dimensional light. The more light you seek, the more adapting your physical body must do. The first step to this adaptation process is to observe your physicality after attending any kind of light activation or upgrade. At first you may feel some exhilaration or light feelings but over time during the repetitive process of communicating with your dimensional self, you may feel fatigue. That is your sign that you may need an energy balancing or adjustment from an energy practitioner. Assistance can also come from wisdom from your multi-dimensional guide who can help you assimilate the light in a meditative state. Taking care of your physical body with self-care practices such as a nap, a soothing bath or nutritious foods can help speed the process along. At any time, you can modulate the light by your intention. You always have the choice to slow the amount of light in this process until you feel fully ready for more integration. The second step in adaptation to the light is to ask yourself what feelings, beliefs or thought forms are coming up to the surface for you to review. Are there patterns of thinking you must let go of or experiences that were hidden away until the proper time for their release? If so, there is no judgment of this as all will be released in the perfect timing for your evolution. Some beliefs and past experiences may easily fade away into the light others show up more than once. But rest assured all will be revealed when you are fully ready to let go and allow the light to transform the old stored energy. Again, working with a practitioner trained in energy release and behavior patterning can enhance this process. The final step is to become aware of the results, what works best for you and when to ask for support. Reaching out to others that are also walking the ascension process is vital. Sharing ascension experiences with others and assisting others in their process can keep your vibration in the light. You then are establishing a new normal for yourself as you find yourself surrounded by others seeking their light. Light attracts light and together you help each other diminish the doubt which is inherent in this type of transformation.

The Language of Light

Your dimensional layers have great capacity for holding light and can be activated in a variety of ways. This activation can come from energetic components such as sound, words, symbology and light projection otherwise known as the language of light. Pay attention to what methods seem to activate your light and give you a sense of peace. The feeling of peace is your barometer to how you assimilate light and store it in your physical body. These methods can correspond with your 5 senses. Through your auditory sense you can process light using particular high vibration sounds or energy patterning. On a scale of 1-5, a simple song that resonates with you and brings you emotional happiness could be a 1, where intuitive guided sound played from the multi-dimensional self, using instruments like a crystal bowl could vibrate at a 5. Instrumental sound has been an ancient bridge that has had a deep potential to connect the human consciousness. In fact, sound can lay the ground work for moving towards a unity consciousness. It even becomes more valuable as one heeds the dimensional guidance to play from a place of intuitive spontaneity. Using these sounds can give you a light vibration that is beneficial for your body and dimensional self, however, not all sounds offer the same amount of light. When working to bridge your human experience with your multi-dimensional self, using the highest vibrational quality of sound will maximize the light transference between the two.

Sound

One of your strongest senses is your auditory capabilities. Through the use of sound, you can instantly change your vibratory flow to intensify or slow the speed of your energy. When working with your multi-dimensional light, sound patterns and tones can be helpful to communicate with this part of yourself. It is not about musicality but vibration and the speed of the flow that is important. Songs are energy patterns too and have the capability of influencing your mood. These types of vibrations serve the mental and emotional bodies and are creations from the physicality of you. Connecting to sounds that mimic nature or from instruments that have been deliberately created for connecting to higher consciousness carry a much different vibration. These instruments have been designed to allow a more receptive state of awareness with your light and dimensional self. Not only are these instruments developed with this intention but they are usually made from natural earth-based materials such as crystals, animal skin or wood. These materials add a resonance with the earth that not only connect you with your own light but the light of the ascending earth. Song and musicality ignite the physical body for human expression. Repetitive vibrations based on high vibration instruments designed for conscious awareness ignite the dimensional self through an unstoppable flow of light. There are times where you need both song and high vibration instruments depending on your evolutionary growth and choices at the moment. Adding a bit of introductory high vibration sound from earth-based instruments can heighten your meditative time and ease you into a multi-dimensional space much quicker than silence. For a richer multi-dimensional experience during your meditation times, start with a few minutes of high vibration sound before entering into your natural silent state. Sound invites the light in and enhances your intention to communicate with your dimensional self. It jumpstarts the energetic flow and increases the familiarity of the light you carry. For those who are drawn to work with these sounds to assist others, there are multi-dimensional guides waiting to share their universal wisdom to expand your natural capability. This opens up yet another telepathic flow that will speed the ascension journey along for all of humanity. Reaching others through the 5 senses as in using sound is a primary step in developing the multi-dimensional pathways you need. The 5 senses can be a useful gateway that enhances your intuitive skill set. To receive the light vibration through sound is a gift you possess and it is waiting to be accessed by your multi-dimensional self. Feed yourself the energy of sound not only through human music but from the high vibration light that is ready to communicate with your dimensional self as well.

Words

Sound is a powerful light activator and comes not just from instruments but from the spoken word which is another component of the language of light. Specific words carry a vibration because of their agreed upon meanings in a given culture. These words have taken on a vibration that has been molded by the human experience and energy of beliefs that surround them. Words are an interpretation at best that can serve to elevate the vibration of energy or to hinder it. They are also filtered by the voice of the user. For example, telling

a story in a monotone voice with little enthusiasm
with high vibration words could be a 1, telling the
same story with light-filled enthusiasm could be a 3.
Using the same high vibration words from the
multi-dimensional self is a 5. All methods transmit
light but not to the same capacity. The human
auditory capacity is a great tool for reaching out and
communicating with the multi-dimensional self.
Your culture revels in the spoken word, the ability
to create imagery from these words and the
emotional waves that they can elicit in the listener.
Both auditory sound whether it comes from the
spoken word or instrumental sound can carry light
vibrations that assist in the ascension process. To
maximize light transference, these auditory factors
need to be considered; the agreed upon meaning of
the words, the intuitive nature of the
instrumentation and the multi-dimensional place of
origin. Where the light vibrations originate is key to
seeking your dimensional self and anchoring that
knowing of self to your human self. Begin by
looking to your multi-dimensional self and holding
the intention that you desire the greatest amount of
light transference you are capable of at the present
time.

Symbology

The energy patterns of specific images or symbols is yet another component of the language of light. Symbols pack a punch with their potential for activating and opening doorways of light within your multi-dimensional self. Whether you view them, draw them or meditate with them, you are acquiring universal truths and a maximum amount of light transference. Symbology is the language of the universe and it promotes a true understanding when receiving telepathic waves of light. The use of symbols can speed your assimilation of light by giving you a potent download of energy that bypasses your mental constructs. In other words, you can choose a laborious method of reading an entire book of words or you can interact with one symbol. Additionally, the energy is transferred without interference from human beliefs or experiences that could interfere with the clarity of the truth. Since ancient times, symbols have been an important part of humanity's evolution and will continue to be useful in the ascension process. In fact, many will be drawn to channel forth new symbols to aide in bridging the gap between the human and dimensional selves. These new symbols will help speed the remembrance and integration of telepathic communication furthering the pathways of energy for use by multi-dimensional guides. Symbols will continue to remain a light-filled potential of energy that are a necessary tool when on the road to ascension.

Light Projection

The light can serve your humanness in many ways. One such avenue is through the intentional sending of light energy to another which is the ultimate component of the language of light. Whether it is hands on or remote projection, the intention to send and emit light is always available. You are meant to be a carrier and transmitter of light. Again, projecting intentional light is yet another way to bridge the gap between the multi-dimensional and human self. As a human you express your light by emotions and physical gestures but as a dimensional being you express light by intentional projection. Linking up to the dimensional self and purposefully sending light is a powerful mechanism to spread your light and help clear the collective consciousness. Intentional projection of light can assist you in attracting more light. It can become a barrier to unwanted energies coming your way. Although it isn't a protection mechanism per se, it can act like one. For instance, if you project a forceful light energy from your dimensional self, immediately you are surrounded by intense light that does not attract anything but pure light. Becoming aware of this ability decreases the fear energy and increases your confidence to go forward with new experiences. The projection of light illuminates the darkness of vulnerability and attracts to you what is necessary for your light filled creations. Beaming light to the collective consciousness can help break up fearful thought forms. Those thought forms that are ready to be transformed by the light will change. Imagine you are walking on a thirsty planet and you have the ability to shower the earth with water. You carry a never-emptying container of water that at will you can saturate every dry piece of land, flower bed and tree. The water is always available to you and you can change a dry landscape into a lush tropical paradise. In your human reality you are on a thirsty planet. The earth and its inhabitants are thirsty for the light you carry. The light energy you radiate is the basic water that is needed for you to transform the collective consciousness, to assist others in their assimilation of light and to emit the strong light that you need to ricochet light back to you. The life cycle needs the light cycle.

Light Codons

The chakra system is an energy system for the human energy field that encompasses the mental, emotional and physical bodies. It is a direct link to your consciousness or the deep wisdom you carry as a human. It has served the consciousness for eons to help balance and stabilize the release of old unwanted energy replacing it with higher vibration energy. The chakra system, however, does not advance your connection to the multi-dimensional system. That is where the light codon system comes in. There is a system within you that has always been there but has been in relative hibernation until this time of evolution. This system is made up of layers upon layers of light codons or points of light that connect you to the dimensional self. Becoming aware of this system and working with it is necessary for the ascension path. It's time to switch over to a new system of light and upgrade the human with the dimensional self. This is a process best done by working with the light codons, activating and feeding them light energy. As the light codons come online, expanding into their light with balance, a new pathway of communication is established. This is where telepathy and clarity of universal wisdom becomes possible. The most direct connection to your multi-dimensional self is through the solar plexus codon. This large and ever-expanding light center is a gateway to your dimensional layers of light. This is a good starting point for the entire system of codons. This system has its own unique pathways that connect the codons making it possible for the light to flood the body. These pathways are called the Matrix of Light system.

Energy Self-Care

Although there are energy practitioners that are ready and able to give you the energetic support you need, it is paramount that you learn some energy self-care. There are easy ways to activate and balance your light to maximize your forward progress on the ascension path. It begins by thinking about "light" or speaking the word "light" which can spark an activation within you. Focusing on this simple word can raise your vibration and help you assimilate more light. This can be done for any amount of time you have available. Remember, the more attention you direct to the word "light," the more light you attract. Relaxing in a quiet space with the intention to balance the energy in your body can be another way to facilitate the equilibrium you seek. Looking at images that help you feel peaceful, loving and connected to the light can facilitate a gentle release of energies that are discordant to your light. Calling on your multi-dimensional guide for light support can further enhance your day-to-day awareness and the activation of your dimensional self. This can be established as a routine during your meditation practice. Physical exercise like walking, yoga or jogging can be enriched by visualizing your multi-dimensional light leaving light-filled footsteps as you connect to the earth. Directing light to another person is yet another way to live in your own light. When others reach out to you for support or assistance, supplement your aid by sending light. Sending light takes no special training to be effective. It comes from having the intention to have someone receive the vibration of light. Whether you imagine bathing someone in a bubble of light or visualize a steady stream of flow moving toward them, light can travel at your request. How you send it is not as important as your intention to send it. Do not let your doubt keep you from sending the light to others and receiving that light in return. Formalize a habit that feels good and makes sense to you. The sending of light can always be the answer as it cannot harm. It is the gift of potential and it serves to facilitate a higher vibration of consciousness.

24/7 Meditation

As you move along your ascension path, you may find that it is not necessary to maintain your regular meditation routine. There will be plenty of times during the ascension process where you just can't sit still or relax enough to go within. As your normal meditation practice starts to shift, you will know that you are connecting more and more to your multi-dimensional self. This dimensional part of you is alive and open to the telepathic transmissions that may be waiting for you. You may have the sudden urge to stop what you are doing and download a concept or send light to another. The multi-dimensional self needs no structure of certain times or repetition. Its available and the blinking open sign is always beckoning the universe for more universal wisdom and light. Of course, you can shut down any energy that wants to come through but why shun the light. Walking the ascension path requires more and more light to assist you to that wholeness you seek. Taking in as much light as the physical body can withstand and balance is the key. There is a lot of shifting going on in this process and it takes some awareness of your mental constructs to become conscious of where you are in the process. The telepathic process of receiving information can defy the linear desire to accept information on a human timeline. Your dimensional self knows what is best for you and will download the light energy at the correct intervals. You will experience that which you need for your evolution. You may go weeks without regular meditation and suddenly you feel the urge to sit quietly and engage with your multi-dimensional self. You may be guided to go to a practitioner or attend a class and the light that has been downloaded is quickly disseminated and balanced into your body. You must let yourself flow with the light and not restrain yourself by false structures put in place to limit the light by your humanness. Do not judge these times of rebellion where you simply cannot be bothered to sit still for 20 or 30 minutes. Know that when you work with your dimensional self that you are engaging constantly in the light and you can let go of any rigid parameters. There are times where you may feel too detached or a bit lost energetically, those are the times it is good to go within with a specific intention to commune with your light. It is not about have to; it is about willingness. It is not about obligation; it is about joyful reunion with the light flow of your own dimensional self. As you continue to bridge the gap between the multi-dimensional self and the human existence, you will find yourself in a constant state of 24/7 meditation. In this state, you are available to the light and universal truths while simultaneously walking and engaging in human pursuits. This is the example of an advanced human existence. This existence actualizes the light and lives by the laws and truths of the universe by constantly receiving light and beaming out light as a participant in unity consciousness.

Energy Machine

Your human form is like an energy machine that is always turned on to emit energy in every second of your existence. How you manipulate and work with that energy creates your reality. Deliberately transmitting the energy that will lead you to a fulfilling and joyful life is key to managing your multi-dimensional light through your human energy machine. You now have more energy to work with and great care must be taken as you express this dimensional light you possess. Using your human consciousness and your existing energy field can be a slow and laborious process. Creating from this place can take months, years or decades to be realized on the 3-d earth plane and to become a part of your day-to-day reality. However, using your multi-dimensional light and creating specifically from those dimensions can speed the process up considerably. Your intention must be clear. We repeat your intention must be clear when creating in this way. Your dimensional self is a jet pack of light energy in a concentrated form. You must learn to wield this new found power responsibly by following the principle of the win-win in a place of unity consciousness. What you create is part of a bigger synchronistic dance of energy where your creation not only serves you but serves others in the process. This is different from the human creation energy in the 3-d plane where individual creations can hinder or hurt others in the process of serving the individual. In other words, multi-dimensional creating can serve the individual but it also serves many at the same time. Following the synchronistic flow of energy makes this possible. It does not require pushing and forcing something to appear but waiting patiently until the correct flow of win-win energy is established to bring about the desired results. Allowing this flow is paramount to the happiness you seek. Waiting for synchronicity may sound like a laborious process but it is just the opposite. It is energetically more efficient because it does not allow the interference of mental and emotional blocks that come from tightly held belief patterns. Furthermore, synchronicity is the basic manifestation process of the dimensional self and the creative energy of those living on an ascended planet. This is how unity consciousness is sustained through this type of energy creating patterns. Imagine if you will, that the happiness you seek through your creative dimensional energy is also the fuel for others to realize their own happiness. It is not only possible but it is a guiding principle of universal intelligence. Your human machine can be upgraded to emit multi-dimensional light through the ascension process which results in actualizing energy in an entirely new way. This new way can connect you to a vast potential of synchronistic flow that guides you to the light of unity consciousness.

Synchronicity

Your multi-dimensional self is wired to flow with the light of synchronicity. This flow is not based on linear time but on the creative light of the universe. The linear time flow is subject to obstacles arising from the collective consciousness that can result in an uphill battle for creating desires. The multi-dimensional self can bypass these obstacles when directly connecting to the light of all universal creation. This sparks the flow of synchronicity bringing forth the attractive energies that you seek in perfect timing. Following linear time is necessary to a point for the human experience but it can also sow the seeds of doubt. When you hold the expectation that something you desire is to show up in particular linear time and not in grand universal time, it can leave you doubting your creative abilities. Your world is full of choice points that are constantly being made that alter creation. What may be possible now, may not be possible seconds from now. The planet of free will and free choice can make the creative process tricky for the human desires. You are choosing, others are choosing and the collective is influencing choice as well. There is also retraction or calling back that which you desire. If something you desire does not show up in your linear time frame, you judge it to be not so and negate the choice. You have chosen something else; you have chosen doubting your own creative abilities. When you are in your flow of multi-dimensional light, you let go of linear time and flow with the synchronicity of the universe. There is inherent ease in this process as your desires show up before you can judge and negate them. When the energy is flowing you stay with your original choice and you are not deterred by doubt. All flows forward in the perfect timing of when you are ready to receive and take appropriate action. Although you may have had these types of experiences without consciously connecting with your dimensional self, they may have been sporadic and a surprising event. For the multi-dimensional-self it is commonplace to live in a place of constant synchronicity. There is ease, trust and confidence to creating your desires from this flow of light. It is the process you were always meant to use.

Prove It

The more time you spend outside of your human experience and commune with your multi-dimensional self, you will know the truth of it. The need for proof is alive and well in all of you. You seek to validate that which is new and seems too easy. Your lessons and experience from the collective consciousness has led you to believe that nothing comes without struggle. A common collective belief is that too much positive emotion could spell trouble as disappointment is the end result. The more you follow that unconscious belief, the more you create it to be so; which takes us back to proof or validation, entering into something new leaves you skeptical and ultimately unsure of yourself. This skepticism can give you the opportunity to re-evaluate both your conscious and unconscious beliefs. It also allows you to be swayed by the collective consciousness and the opinions of others; the perfect storm of sowing the seeds of doubt, leaving you paralyzed on your path to ascension. Doubt eats away at your spiritual strength until you are no longer connected to the truth of you. Doubt is the obstacle you must overcome not fear. When you doubt your light, you doubt the very essence of you and block the connection to the multi-dimensional self. You are aware of your fears but are you aware of your doubt to the light you are? Ponder this concept of doubt. Working toward removing it, will give you all the proof you need to go forward. As you get to know your dimensional self and energetically travel within it, you will begin to know your truth which lessens the need for validation of your experiences. It's simply about your intention to go forward and practice that which you already are.

Confidence

As your connection to the collective consciousness becomes diminished, you will find yourself needing more reassurance to stabilize your energy. Untethering from the collective will seem uncomfortable at times until you replace the antiquated beliefs and distorted thought forms with universal truth. You will begin to meld your own mental process with your intuitive feelings fed by your dimensional self. You will step into a wholeness that you have not experienced before. Your dimensional self becomes the facilitator of light energy that takes the place of collective agreements that no longer serve your evolutionary growth. These collective patterns are not who you are but something you have been taught to substitute for the reunification of your multi-dimensional light. These patterns have given you a false confidence that only works by following the beliefs of the many which stunts real evolutionary growth. Once you start experiencing the wholeness and light that you are, however, you will build a new type of confidence that truly originates from within. You in essence become unshakeable in your journey to express your light. You will not be easily influenced by others or the energies that do not serve your ascension process. This may take time. This is why we call it an ascension process. Taking the necessary steps forward in full awareness and living in a trusting state of light builds genuine confidence. Replace the familiarity of being an unaware follower of the collective consciousness with the true knowing of your vast creative light. This awareness and knowing of your wholeness is the keys to residing in the confident light that you are.

In Conclusion

You are the light you have been looking for and that connection is through your multi-dimensional self. Now is the time for you to explore and experience this part of yourself that has been waiting for this time of ascension for both the planet and humanity. The support for knowing yourself in this way is seeded deep into your energy fields waiting for the signal from you to turn the lights on. Your dimensional self is like a room that has never been used but is nonetheless unique in its potential to offer the space to once again seek your expanded abilities and purpose for existence. Through this book and many others, you will be given the information to utilize and express the light that you are. You will take the next step in truly knowing yourself as an energetic being that wears the human cloak of physicality and consciousness. Together these parts of yourself will help actualize an emerging new world and the anchoring of unity consciousness. In time, you will come to understand how important your light is in operating the creative engine that you are. Universal intelligence and truth will be your focus as you take your place as a citizen of the universe. But most importantly, you will be the sovereign being of energy you have longed to be and this comes with knowing your own light. The multi-dimensional self is the gateway to the freedom from separation and limiting beliefs of an old consciousness. It provides the platform for infinite possibilities and expressions of light that only you can create. In this time of ascension, re-acquaint yourself with your potential of light that is your multi-dimensional self. Allow yourself to explore this room of possibilities and creative energy to further your own evolution and by doing so you join all of us light beings in the expansion of universal unity.

The Multi-Dimensional Energy

The multi-dimensional self sees itself as energy whereas the human self sees itself as flesh and bones. The workings of the human self whether it be mental, emotional or physical is in essence creative energy in motion. Although, through the lens of the 5 senses it is looked upon as solid matter, it still remains energy. So, imagine if you will that you are spinning a plate full of energy, constantly keeping it in motion for your survival and your expression. Your human existence up to this point has had this singular focus of one dinner plate. With the awakening of your multi-dimensional self, you now have the opportunity to spin a complete set of dinner plates full of energy. This energy is not only for your expression through the human experience but to advance you through your next evolution. In some respects, it is about survival because evolution is synonymous with adaptation, realization and expansion. The exploration of your multi-dimensional self is experiencing not one plate of energy but all the plates of energy potential that are at your disposal. Therefore, it is helpful to look at your world from the lens of creating energy, expressing energy and exchanging energy. The ascension journey awakens you to the responsibility you have to wield your energy within the framework of the consciousness of unity not separation. The journey ahead of you is challenging you to multi-task your energy back and forth between many plates of energy. Your original plate of energy continues to anchor you to the earth while you explore and become familiar with the many plates of energy that is your wholeness. This exploration comes through multi-dimensional travel, telepathy and a greater understanding of your energetic field. It is now time to start to ponder deeply how you express your energy and how these expressions echo back at you in your reality. The concept of energy expression is vast but looking at your world through the lens of energy serves many purposes. One important purpose is the viewpoint that everything is energy assists you in detaching from the collective consciousness. When examining a situation from this viewpoint, you do not get distracted by beliefs and old thought forms instead you can instantly gain a fresh perspective. Secondly, this viewpoint can help neutralize emotions that may cloud your thinking or promote unnecessary reactions. And finally, this viewpoint will assist you in cultivating the habits of living from your own truth and not the collective. This promotes confidence in your abilities and paves the way for creating from the light that you are. The potential of energy that has laid dormant within you until now is wonderous and is your direct link back to the light of your origin. Learning to spin the many plates of your energy potential is what the ascension journey is all about. Integrating and expressing this energetic potential while still walking the journey of being a human is your next evolutionary step.

Multi-Dimensional Travel

Your human existence as a creator of your experiences and the expansion of your energy springs forth from the overwhelming need to explore. All of you are explorers in some sense of the word; utilizing your 5 senses to quench your curiosity and awaken your consciousness. Whether you travel far and wide or stay close to where you reside, you are still the explorer of your world. The ascension journey, however, requires you to travel within instead of outside yourself. Your multi-dimensional energy becomes your vehicle to explore the many dimensions of yourself that are ready to be discovered. And oh, what a vehicle it is, taking you to the ultimate experience of exploration. This vehicle is fueled by your focus to activate and assimilate light. Therefore, the more fuel, the more possibilities open up to you to become closer to the origin of your light and your connection to universal truths. These discoveries and many others come from experiencing this part of yourself by your travel within. You begin to familiarize yourself with the potential of these layers when you flow with your multi-dimensional energy. It is much like entering a jet stream allowing yourself to be propelled to those dimensional places that most benefit you. It is not quantified in miles but in the quality of your experiences and what is suitable at that time for your development and growth. Additionally, multi-dimensional travel can serve as a gateway to the infinite possibilities of connecting to all life in the universe. It enables you to receive the necessary support from those light beings that are in service to the ascension process, thus, bypassing the human language and it's constructs that lack the necessary vibrations to promote the true understanding of universal truths. Instead, you gain a dimensional perspective that not only facilitates your energetic expansion but paves the way for telepathy. Communication from multi-dimensional travel is your next step and is accessed by flowing within your jet stream of light.

Telepathy with your Multi-Dimensional Guides

Telepathy is the preferred method of communication used by multi-dimensional light guides. Light language and the frequency thereof is universal and does not need translation. Light is light and cannot be easily distorted by beliefs and mental thought forms. Symbols are an example of how an entire download of universal wisdom can be conveyed and be used to activate the light centers of the dimensional self. This is much more efficient than trying to communicate via a long energetic process. By allowing yourself to work with the various vibrations of telepathic light, your dimensional self can once again remember and assimilate universal intelligence. Working with multi-dimensional guides takes practice but the rewards are many. Your evolution is sped up because you can quickly bridge that gap between your human existence and your multi-dimensional self. Your connection to the ascending earth expands and you learn how to assist the earth by anchoring your universal light in various ways.

Furthermore, you begin to experience unity consciousness as more than a concept because the multi-dimensional guides exist in this consciousness.

Energy Interference

When working with multi-dimensional guides, it is prudent to ask for one spokesperson to assist you. The universe is teeming with light beings that will be of service to you in a variety of ways. Universal intelligence has been waiting a long time for humanity to wake up to this ascension process and it can't be overstated, their energies are eager to assist. However, during the discovery phase when building a bridge between your dimensional self and your humanness, great care must be taken to keep the physical body in balance. By allowing numerous energies to influence your field, you could easily be confused about how to be purposeful in your service to the earth and all of humanity. Even if your purpose is to work with many different types of light beings, all connection should be done through one reliable source, with whom you have built a trusting relationship. Over time that one connection may shift but, in the beginning, to safely protect your physical body, its best to rely on one multi-dimensional guide. Now many will have guides that come forth in a trinity or a collective of energies which is common for universal intelligence. Unity consciousness is the way of the universe and it is natural for light beings to gather in groups of energies. However, in this scenario there is one voice being projected. One being may be the designated communicator or the collective will channel their energies as one which makes it seem it is one voice. The reason for this is twofold; one you are familiar with communicating as an individual not as a collective group and secondly, when using telepathic flow, the light energy emitted is easily balanced and in alignment with the physical body. We cannot stress enough the consideration that must be taken to safeguard your physicality in this time of transition. Every day your body is being bombarded by a chaotic energy that is bubbling out of the collective consciousness and influencing the emotional and mental bodies. This is combined with the energy of your planet whose magnetics and dimensional familiarity has changed. Just these two factors can be an energetic overload which is only compounded when you start traveling your ascension path. This changing reality you find yourself in makes it imperative to rely on creating a trusting relationship with a multi-dimensional light being who can be your true guide to universal intelligence. Working toward building that foundation of trust and familiarity will not only speed the ascension process but shield your physical body from more wear and tear.

Citizen of the Universe

What does it take to be a citizen of the universe you might ask? First and foremost, it is the awareness that the universe is alive and teeming with life. Humanity has been easily led astray by the myopic vision that the earth is a singular place where the only intelligent life exists. The sky serves as your gateway to the universe and it is too far away from the everyday existence that humans lead. Many past cultures saw themselves as one with the universe seeing their part as a component of the whole but that is not the case for modern cultures. Yes, there are still pockets of civilizations that have held on to their links with universal intelligence but they are few and far between. The average human only thinks of the universe in terms of a sky full of warm sunlight, twinkling night stars and weather. Humanity's remembrance of their true connection to the universe is long gone. Occasionally, during technological advances with space travel and satellite photos, humans are once again reminded of their link to the universe but only in competitive and exploitative ways with little thought to the true meaning of life. Furthermore, what is not easily visible or experienced is easily discarded or relegated to the laborious process of proof. For most of humanity the universe is a big unknown which can pose a problem when the human survival instincts trigger you to fear the unknown. To fully participate as a universal citizen, you must be open to those life forms that do not look, behave or exist as you do. You can see that this poses a challenge for humanity due to an existing world where humans are scrutinized and categorized in various ways that keep you separate from each other. How can you possibly relate to life forms that are far different than you when you cannot relate to your fellow humans who are you. Your evolutionary process is urging you to move in a direction of acceptance and tolerance for that which is different from you. Right now, the human separation is glaringly apparent, but over time the energy of the ascension process will facilitate inclusiveness and unity. Being reunited with your multi-dimensional self will assist you in purging this collective fear you carry based on past information that has always been filtered through the human lens of separation. When you view the universe from your dimensional self and not your human self, the fear drops away and you experience the truth of participating as a universal citizen. This citizenship cannot be realized from the human state of mind but it can be actualized by the dimensional self.

Seeking Us

It is rather laughable that humanity spends so much time and money to look for us out in the cosmos. Although it is instinctual to look towards the stars for greater meaning and intelligence, it is pure folly to seek us through the 3-d lens on which your reality is based on. Your machines and devices to detect life out in the universe are created and developed through your 5 senses influenced by the collective consciousness of evidence-based science. You look for proof of a dimensional world through the filter of your human experience and 5 senses. Evidence is subject to the tangible 3-d world you are creating not from not the dimensional world of the light. We reside in that dimensional world not your 3-d world so true communication and connection must be made through your dimensional self. We are out there we assure you but we are not willing to reside in the density of your 3-d world. We do not operate from 5 senses but rely on telepathy to communicate with others like us. We are one in the light and will become apparent to you when you work with the light of your multi-dimensional self. When you seek your light, you will find your light and all the various light beings of the universe. We are not hiding from you; you are hiding from us by not awakening to your true calling. We have been waiting for your call as seekers of multi-dimensional light. We are not interested in conversing with your 3-d machinery or your closed logical minds, we are interested in much more. We are here to assist you with your maturity to become a citizen of the universe and to truly know your light. Unfortunately, your 3-d exploration is based on competition, ownership and colonization, energies that have served you in the past but do not serve you now. These energies are not of the unity consciousness that you are evolving into nor are they supported by universal intelligence. To be a true explorer of what the cosmos holds, you must think outside of the box by not relying on the old collective consciousness to show you the way. Look to your dimensional self to illuminate your path and join others in their ascension journey. It does not take a space ship to discover the gateways to higher dimensional intelligence. It takes the willingness to once again connect with your light and all the possibilities you can create. Do not look up, look inward as you once again become familiar with this part of you that is the explorer who becomes a true citizen of the universe. You will find us waiting in the light.

In Conclusion

Part of the ascension process is once again connecting to and communicating with universal intelligence through your multi-dimensional energy. In this process, you are aware of your light capabilities and that awareness is the hallmark of participating in a meaningful way as a citizen of the universe. It is all about the light and your quest to know your light-filled dimensional self. As you become reacquainted with this dimensional part of yourself, you begin to take the necessary steps to fulfill your destiny as a universal citizen. The blinders drop away and you reimagine a life where the earth is one important component along with many others in the vastness of dimensional space. The earth is no longer central; it is a collaborative partner with all the various life forms of an alive and awake universe. Your planet no longer becomes an experimental lab where it is observed but not taken seriously. As your consciousness explodes fully into ascension awareness, you guide humanity and your planet to take a meaningful part in the cosmic web of light. This is what you were always meant to do and you get there by acknowledging the truth that you are much more than your human existence; you are the light you seek.

Unity Consciousness

Unity consciousness is the way of the new world where humanity resides on a new vibrational earth. This is the consciousness that the earth will support and embody, the light of universal truths. The breakdown of the collective consciousness is paving the way for humanity's existence to once again become connected to truth and not antiquated belief systems. Within the collective there are truths that will be propelled forward into the new consciousness; truths that have been covered over by years of human experiences. This evolutionary process of a transforming collective consciousness to unity conscious is ongoing until eventually all join in this new web of energy. The purity of this new energy enables the complete connection between the multi-dimensional and human selves. Many are already breaking free of the old collective and slowly recognizing the need for unity consciousness. It has been a dream for many to live by an expression of energy that facilitates a win-win for all of humanity. This dream is coming to fruition with the awakening of the multi-dimensional self and contact with universal truths. Unity consciousness knows no limitations or separation from the origin of light. It is the human experience of knowing its full potential of light and creating from it. Unity consciousness, however, is not to be confused with Christ consciousness which has been the embodiment of the ascension of a few. Christ consciousness is an energy of potential and possibility but not the end collective result. It was a demonstration of what could be through an agreed upon master that knew their light. Unity consciousness is the embodiment of everyone knowing and walking in their light. It is for the whole not the few.

An Experience of Unity

True unity is a consciousness that must be experienced to its fullest through your pathways of light. What you perceive as unity in your human world is but a mere reflection created from various ideologies of belief patterns on your planet. Based on these beliefs, groups form and communities are built from a singular focus. As long as everyone continues to agree to this focus a partial unified field is created. We say partial because wholeness cannot be achieved when you as individuals are disconnected to your own wholeness. Remember you are the creators and the energy you have been creating from has come through the collective consciousness, a place of separation. In other words, you cannot create wholeness when your energy is not whole. At times, you may have had glimpses of what it would feel like to be connected to all that is through the expansion of your own awareness. These moments are fleeting at best but serve as a reminder that you have the ability to connect to your own wholeness. Therefore, the ascension process and knowing your own wholeness through the multi-dimensional self is key to experiencing unity consciousness. Unity is more than a concept and you will realize this potential of energy when humanity begins to know its light. Many are beginning to connect to their light through their dimensional selves as part of the ascension process. When they do this, they start to create from a unified field of wholeness within themselves. This sets a flow of energy in place which is anchored to the earth as unity consciousness. In these beginning stages, you become a creator from both collective consciousness and unity consciousness until you move closer and closer to your wholeness. Eventually, you create from the energy of unity consciousness disconnecting from the collective consciousness while simultaneously expressing this energy through your human existence. Many of you on the ascension path are paving the way for others to feel the effects of this flow of energy that is building in intensity. Your deliberate collaboration with your wholeness through your dimensional self provides the service for others to wake up to their wholeness potential. Therefore, your service is instrumental in establishing a tipping point of light.

The Tipping Point of Light

The buildup of light energy has a tipping point where the flow of light not only accelerates but moves with such a force it cannot be stopped. That is what you see when you watch the changes in your world and the evolution of humanity. As more of you wake up to your light, the energy of ascension cascades forward resulting in a tipping point of transformation. What once was a slow process of 3 steps forward and 2 steps back becomes an overwhelming indelible change. The path becomes clear and humanity becomes ripe to accept and allow that which seemed out of reach. During your ascension journey, you will see many such tipping points enabled by the unifying energy of synchronicity. Humanity's need to unify, which is at the core of your human existence, will activate the collective consciousness to transform itself into unity consciousness. This can be done rapidly due to the energetic tipping points that effect not just the individual but the whole. Many of you have known about the concept of tipping points but up until now this light flow trickled slowly in your linear time. As you discover and work with your multi-dimensional light you will open the flood gates of light energy and actualize many points of collective change. This is fueled by the acceptance of your light and the dimensional being that you are. These tipping points of light are where the peace and the new world you imagine becomes possible.

The Big Benefit

Imagine a world residing in unity consciousness where the uniqueness of each individual is honored and celebrated. In this same world, all live knowing their importance to the earth, each other and to other star systems of light beings. Each individual is supported in their curiosity and development as they create from their supreme wholeness. At the same time their participation with others and the planet supports the entire web of energy of a unified field of existence. One voice becomes the echo of many in resonance with universal truth and light.

The world becomes a place of doing no harm, seeking the light in others and creating from the purity of one's origin. Unity consciousness is the foundation from which humanity can experience and exist in wholeness with the light. Individuals that create from their dimensional light, feed the energy of wholeness in a never-ending cycle of possibilities. Therefore, what benefits the individual becomes the big benefit for all of life on planet earth.

In Conclusion

Unity consciousness is a universal truth and, like many universal truths, they must be experienced to appreciate their full meaning. Language is a poor substitute for the comprehension of a truth that is multi-dimensional in its nature. This truth beckons you to experience this energy and to ponder for yourself the possibilities that are available. By embarking on the ascension path, you are on the road to the wholeness that makes unity consciousness possible. Your participation in seeking your light enables others to do the same which accelerates the flow of energy for this great change. Unity consciousness is the foundation of a new emerging world that needs your full creative abilities in expressing your light. The merging of your dimensional self with your human existence is the catalyst for many universal truths to become anchored and actualized on the planet. Therefore, you become a part of the wholeness of a vast universal web of light and a citizen of the universe. Now is the time to heed the call of your dimensional light by walking the road of ascension. Unity consciousness awaits you.

THE ROAD TO ASCENSION

Part 2

Concepts to Contemplate

In this part of the book, we have given your mind concepts to contemplate that are not only important for your understanding but chosen for their dimensional light. These concepts have the potential to activate your own multi-dimensional energy and stimulate your own inner truth. These concepts have been channeled through in a non-linear time fashion as to best preserve the light-filled energy they possess. As you exercise your mind by reading these words, you will also be receiving the necessary energy and vibration to assist you on your ascension journey. We ask that you take the time to ponder this information and suggested activities at your own energetic pace. The act of pondering stimulates the vibration of carefully considering information before reaching a conclusion. In other words, do these concepts resonate with you, do they feel like your truth and are they in accordance with the way you want to progress. Ponder deeply and richly allowing your own energy vibration to spring forth and give you the validation of your own inner truth.

Universal Light

What if you thought about all life in the universe as light? What if you let go of the notion that life in the universe had to be a humanized form? The human experience labels the universe with its 3-dimensional thinking and the use of the 5 senses. The multi-dimensional part of you sees the universe as light; energies after energies of light. There is automatic tolerance and acceptance of the universe when you perceive is as it is, energies of light. Many in the universe have taken on various containers to appear as more than light. They are trying on a particular form for expression, however, at their very core there is light. In your world, form matters and serves the separation of all of you as your light. When the focus is on form, it detracts from the core of light that you are. Form becomes the ultimate barometer of judgement.

Intention

What is intention? It is a flow of energy light that you can use to create from. Intention is the engine of your creation and it is up to you to dial up the strength and quality of this intention to feed your creative engine. With strong clear intention you can create a synchronicity with the universe. Using this energy when you are in your multi-dimensional self magnifies the creation you seek. In the human state much of the light of intention is filtered. Intention must negotiate the mental and emotional fields which dilute its potency. Thus, you may have to work over and over on a particular intention. However, the light that flows from your multi-dimensional self is pure unfiltered light that can magnify your intention. It is not encumbered with competing energies of a neuro-net of beliefs and thought forms. Therefore, creating with intention from the dimensional self is more efficient and satisfying.

Helping Hand

You are surrounded on your ascension path with assistance in various forms. The ultimate responsibility is yours, however, for the light you seek is within you. It is not a nebulous cloud somewhere that someone or something will give you. You are your own leader with the skills to successfully journey yourself back to your light. You must recognize your leadership by becoming reacquainted with your own connection to the light and by continually activating your light. You must learn to receive wisdom from the universe and ask for support from multi-dimensional light beings who can hold you in a space of light. These light beings have new universal concepts and wisdom to share that comes wrapped in a package of light. This wisdom is the telepathic energy of light and as you receive it you are refreshed and renewed in the light.

God, Source & All That Is

Many of you may be wondering how the concept of God or Source fits into the ascension process and the quest for dimensional light. First, we must be clear that there is no separation between these concepts for they are all a part of the ultimate light and unity of the universe. Your perception of the concept of God or Source has been limited by your attempt at fitting it into a mental 3-d construct. Additionally, your perception has been attached to the structure of hierarchy and systemic judgment within the collective consciousness. The fundamental knowing of God or Source has always been meant to be experienced through the creative light that connects all that is. It is the ultimate consciousness so to speak, pure in its expression and inclusive of all beings in the universe. We as 9th dimensional resident beings are not gods or your greatest source of light. We, like you, are here to experience our light whether it be in service to another planetary system or in our own evolutionary progress. In our own reality, we do not live in a hierarchal system nor do we look upon other universal light beings from that perspective. One light being is not judged over another regardless of their dimensional space of origin or their current evolution. Dimensions are energies to be experienced not to be used to judge another's evolution. Universal life is constantly evolving dimensionally and like you, other light beings are seeking experiences from their true connection to the definitive source of all light.

Choice

One of the greatest gifts that humanity possesses is the ability to choose through their mental thought forms, their emotional reactions and subsequent behaviors. You are wired to be a creator in order to experience your reality through evolutionary growth. This ability comes from using your intention, physical attributes and energetic consciousness. Much of what you choose is heavily influenced by the energy of the collective consciousness. This influence keeps you creating repetitive patterns that erode your confidence as a creator. True freedom of choice comes from your own innate wisdom and light; yet another reason to seek out your dimensional self. By using the gift of choice from the dimensional self, you set your own reality in motion by creating from the uniqueness of your light which then serves your sovereignty. You are no longer on repeat mode from the influence of collective consciousness that has you experiencing the same reactions and behaviors over and over. Therefore, communicating and creating from your multi-dimensional light can offer beneficial choice opportunities that were not easily realized in the past. Choice will remain an option whether through the human experience or through the dimensional self. Choosing from your dimensional light, however, will benefit your ascension journey by maintaining the integrity and individuality energy of your creations. The freedom you seek is waiting in the truth of your light.

Extrasensory Perceptions

Many of you are aware of possessing perceptions far beyond your 5 senses and natural human ability. In the past, these perceptions have not always been looked upon in a favorable way as they do not align well in the collective consciousness world. Clairaudience, clairsentience and clairvoyance to name a few, are all extrasensory perceptions that will expand as you seek your multi-dimensional self. As you open up to the dimensional world with more light, these abilities will bring forth more and more information for you to manage. You may currently know how to manage these abilities by hiding them, ignoring them or acting on them as you see fit. These perceptions will become more prevalent and powerful in your everyday world. The key to this expansion is learning to manage these perceptions as you negotiate a changing world. As the information comes to you, take time to be with the sensations and analyze how they make you feel. By analyzing we do not mean taking apart every nuance but instead weighing the neutrality of the information. The first step when receiving any perception is looking at it from a neutral vantage point. Secondly, journal and document the sensations and the messages that come to you. This is most crucial when receiving visions or information about the future. Remember you are still on a planet of free will and free choice and future events can change due to the choices of others. Acting on this information at the incorrect time can disappoint and frustrate you and sow the seeds of doubt. This doubt blocks your abilities and can skew further information. The third step is weighing how attached you are to the information especially when it is something you desire. Give it time to show itself in your human existence. And finally, communicate with your multi-dimensional guides as how to proceed and whether there are necessary action steps to take. Sometimes you have wisdom that is for just your knowing or only for a specific person. Ask for guidance before taking action steps as dimensional wisdom may not play out in a linear way. Over time you will become confident with the expansion of these abilities and working with them will be another step in bridging the gap between the human and the multi-dimensional self.

Detachment

In the human world, attaching to objects, people and concepts is taught and revered. The further you stray from your inner light, the easier it is to become attached to substitutes for the truth of you. Humanity's separation is a vast gap that is filled every day with the attachments outside of yourself that keep you from your true connection. The energy it takes to attach to the outside world is overwhelming at times. This out go of energy is not natural and it puts stress and strain on the human form. The more you attach the more energy you expend and the further you move from your origin of light. These attachments are fostered early on for example as a child you may have had a favorite toy, family values that were taught to you and later a relationship with another. You are taught to see the world through your attachments. That is why it's imperative to look closely at how you invest your energy and how you hold on to it. Detachment is seen in your world as apathy, separation and indifference. However true detachment that comes from the light of the multi-dimensional self, is just the opposite. When you let go or detach from your outer world, your inner light can serve the world around you. This type of detachment is not a mental process but a dimensional process that uses the light to stabilize and put you in a neutral state. From this neutral state, true compassion, wisdom and truth can pour forth from you because it is not filtered by the distortions of fear. When determining your level of attachment, one only needs to look at the emotional component of that object, person or concept. Using the emotions as your guide, you can ask yourself what amount of fearful energy is wrapped up in this attachment. Is this attachment bringing me struggle or joy?

Separation

Your light bodies are never separated from the whole but your mental constructs mask the truth of this. Your mental process through the human lens shows you where you are separate and is constantly scanning opportunities for this proof or validation that you are an individual. This lens is now open so wide that it cannot see the unity before it. It is on overdrive encouraging your perceptions that you are a separate entity, a false sense of freedom from the unity that is alive and well around you. The more you try to separate yourself from others the further you are away from your true light. However, what is ironic is when you don the container of a human, you must identify first and foremost as an individual. This taking on the human experience cloaks the unity truth that is at your core of existence. You start tipping your scale so that you see only the expansion of your individual choices at the expense of your unity within. This is not to say that you are not a unique individual or a human with a specific purpose for being on earth, it is to say that you are more than that. You are also connected to a unity consciousness, a web of light that is a far greater experience than your projected separate identity.

Laughter

One of the greatest gifts of the human experience is the ability to discharge light through the energy of laughter. In our observation of this gift, we do not focus on the human facial expressions or sounds but the amount of light that explodes forth from this simple action. During the emotional discharge of a laughter event, you are surrounded by the highest vibration of light that has been facilitated by the human and the 5 senses. It is manufactured light from the human experience and it expands the more humans come together to engage in a laughter event. Light pours forth and flows in a swirling pattern engulfing you and titillating your 5 senses. You engage in a magnified sensation of light that can be quite contagious. You spread the light of you through laughter which supports others in their engagement in the light. Although the action of laughter is powerful in itself for changing mood and emotions, the amount of light is small compared to the potential of light coming from your multi-dimensional self. The act of laughter although enjoyable is not an activity you engage in for hours on end. This would be too exhaustive to the body to create and emit the amount of light necessary for true transformation. Imagine if you will, the light of laugher being expanded a million times over, an endless potential of light that is waiting for you through your dimensional self. This is what awaits you by seeking and walking the ascension process. Vast amounts of light are stored in the many dimensions of yourself ready for assimilation and integration. This quality and quantity of light cannot be absorbed without careful measure. Be patient with your physical body and trust that the light will be waiting for you whenever you are ready.

Movement

The physical body is meant to move in a variety of ways for basic survival and for experiencing the world through the 5 senses. This movement capability is a tool to be used by the multi-dimensional self for the true assimilation of light. The energy of light is meant to flow and move through the energy field to partner with creative intention. It is not meant to sit passively by and be stored in a reservoir waiting for emission. The true nature of light is to be in constant motion touching and sparking more light in perfect synchronicity. The physical body can aide in this flow of light by moving in specific ways that can assist in assimilation and activation of the multi-dimensional light. Simply put, concentrate on moving your light energy in unison with deliberate physical actions of your choosing. Many of you may have a physical movement practice that connects you to your own conscious awareness. This practice, including working with the breath, can be amped up by your intention to move with your light. Additionally, during meditation imagine moving your light throughout your body from your light centers. Visualize or sense the light flooding certain organs, muscles and bones in order to promote harmony with the body for greater stamina when participating in the ascension process. Begin to experience how light moves within you by seeking out an energy practitioner that can assist you in this awareness. The key to assimilating light for your benefit is to flow with the innate nature of the light and move with the synchronicity of that expression.

Food for Thought

The collective consciousness is full of thought forms that have guided humanity for eons of time but as you break free from this consciousness what energy takes its place? Your brain is constantly musing about concepts, ideas and opinions of others. Where do you find the purity of thought forms that are the guiding principles of the new world? How do you replace the old thoughts and beliefs with the new universal truths when seeking the light? How do you tap into unity consciousness while still being tethered to the collective? All of these questions are answered when you intentionally communicate with the light through your multi-dimensional self. This light is your energy nutrition that feeds you and transforms the physical, mental and emotional bodies of the human experience. Focusing on the light that you are is key to giving you the "new food for thought". By riding the light through your dimensional self and holding the intention to retain this light, you are prioritizing the thought forms you assimilate. The more your thought forms come from the light, the more the thought forms from the collective are in the background. Over time the collective withers away within you and the light takes its place. A simple exercise is to quiet yourself with the intention to contact your multi-dimensional self and receive the "new food for thought." Imagine a stream of light bringing in the purity of thought forms originating from unity consciousness. You must build a bridge for yourself between the old collective consciousness and the unity consciousness you seek. Working with the multi-dimensional self and the intention to contact these pure light-filled thought forms will over time make universal truth your center of belief. The background noise of the collective will be silenced and clarity is yours. The energy of your nutrition comes from the light and universal truth not antiquated beliefs that guide the collective. You step into unity consciousness each time you bridge this gap between what was and what is. Unity consciousness is here. It has been created and its ready for you to incrementally step into now. Start the process by accepting life force nutrition and stoke your appetite for the light. Devour the light that you are. It's your birthright!

Doubt

Doubt is a form of carrying both the individual and collective vibration of fear. Unlike the emotion of fear, doubt is not clearly visible especially to your conscious mind. We are not talking about lack of confidence but of an intrinsic vibration that is carried deep within that negates the concept of your origin of light. Doubt is everywhere in your world and eats away at your essence; that which you truly are. When pursuing the ascension path, fears arise and blocked energy pours forth for you to transform energetically. Fear is in plain sight as it arouses the 5 human senses of survival. Doubting that you are 100% light is the biggest obstacle to knowing your origin of light. Of course, those reading this book may say that they know they are the light but do you

disappointment influence your creative abilities. Letting go and truly allowing synchronistic moments to appear will bring a renewed energy to your knowing of what is correct for you and your purpose. This is not the release of the outcome but the process of releasing the time intervals you have assigned to such outcomes. This is important learning because as you open up to the light your dimensional wisdom will be unlocking a flood of energetic information. When to act on this information or create something from it, is answered by following the synchronistic flow of universal light not human time lines. This is challenging for your human existence as all your beliefs and agreements have been predicated on time intervals. It is the unlearning process to not hold on tightly to specific actions based on time. What you may call divine timing is a synchronistic flow of energy that attracts all of the pieces of light that make up the intended creation. Imagine a jigsaw puzzle where all the pieces magically fall into place in one moment instead of being scattered about laboriously looking for the next piece to fit. In your physicality of being a human you would slowly pick up each piece one after another trying to complete the puzzle. Sometimes the pieces fit together quickly others are discarded and another piece is tried. This is a linear time process. However, in your multi-dimensional self, the pieces are still scattered about but stay waiting for that one synchronistic flow of energy to attract them together and complete the puzzle. This flow of energy is true perfection and what was once a puzzle is now a creation of clarity. Puzzles engage the mind with a lot of head scratching and doubt. Creations of clarity engage the consciousness and offer the opportunity for confident satisfying actions. There are no regrets when using synchronistic flow. This flow provides perfect timing and win-win solutions that are deeply rooted in unity consciousness. Your dimensional self knows how to work with this flow and should be called upon whenever your intention is to create clarity, confident actions and light-filled solutions.

Namaste

Ancient truths have been seeded on your planet from various spiritual traditions. The concept of namaste is one of these truths and is used symbolically in recognizing light or consciousness in another. In your daily world you look no further than assessing the human container for various flaws, similarities and emotional connections. These types of assessments reduce human interactions into various categories that foster separation.

However, the multi-dimensional self cannot be so easily categorized. On the surface, the multi-dimensional self is simply your light and true connection to the pure truth of who you are. In the new world this concept of namaste becomes heighted to the connection of that purity of light that you are. You acknowledge another not only in respect to their consciousness but to the pure light of their origin. This supports unity consciousness and an elevated human experience. There is no assessment needed as one perceives another from a place of light. This makes it easier to see another as they really are instead of the various categories and judgments of the collective consciousness.

Starlight

At first you must use your 5 senses to engage in your connection to your multi-dimensional self whether it be through auditory or visual pathways as well as your breath. Using your visual capacity is a strong way to access your light through the power of imagination. Remembering images you have seen in the past can be helpful in moving your energy to that natural flow of light you possess. One such image that can be extremely helpful is recalling a night sky full of stars. Starlight is another form of creative light and just the idea of it can foster your creative flow. Starlight can hold the purity of birthing something new and unique. These images of the stars and the constellations that you are familiar with can remind you of your own purity of origin. Like a sky full of stars, you too have the capacity for evolving in the light with infinite possibilities. Focus on one-star constellation that you are intrigued with and imagine interacting with that light. Ask yourself why you are drawn to this particular formation of stars? The answer may surprise you.

Words

Language is an important component to the collective consciousness. Each word spoken no matter the culture emits a vibration that finds its way into the collective. It is not about the meaning as much as it is about the specific vibration. Words have held humanity hostage perpetuating the beliefs of a collective past of struggle and suffering. Even words that you may think of as positive affirming words will no longer be applicable in the new world. Let's take the word "mercy" which is believed to be such a positive word and has its roots in a spiritual context. "Mercy" suggests that there is some type of oppression or trauma invoked on someone so that they must ask for "mercy."

Through this word, one is asking for leniency, less pain or a suppression of low vibration energy. Invoking such a word vibration potentiates the energy of struggle and suffering. In the new world, there is no need for "mercy" as the energy of oppression has been transmuted from power over to power to. It is easy to consider those word vibrations that appear negative or low vibration but also ponder those words that may be a counter-balance like "mercy." Weigh if you will the vibration of the words you speak not only on a scale of high/low vibration feelings but their appropriateness in a new world based on unity consciousness. Ask yourself which words are no longer relevant and can be purged from the collective consciousness. In the new world there exists a vibration of truth which your language will eventually evolve to. There will be less word vibration and more understanding through telepathic communication. Words and the language they serve will evolve as humanity evolves. In the meantime, consider the vibration of the words you speak in the context of how you might operate in the new world. Bring forth the vibration of unity consciousness through your language and focus on the true meaning of your speech. Uplift your language by letting go of those words that hold you back from your birthright of ascension.

Ride the Tide

The discovery of your multi-dimensional self can add a layer of uncertainty when living in the 3-d human container of your existence. Often you will ride the tide of emotions, mental constructs and physical sensations that may be confusing or even throw you off balance. This energetic movement as you build your bridge of light between your dimensional self and human self can also be influenced by the outward forces at work in your world. This can be challenging at times as you seek to restore what is always familiar to you when you work with your energetic self. Your world is like a ship which rolls from side to side with each upcoming wave. The waves consist of the clash between two opposing vibrations; an ascending planet and the collective consciousness. Adding to that you are becoming more sensitive to the many dimensional changes within you as you grow into the ascension energy. This extreme motion can catch you off guard at times and have you seeking some peace and refuge. At this time of extreme transition, you must be vigilant in the care of your energetic field and the pace at which you move forward. Once you start assimilating more light, you will desire to have more light and more interactions with your dimensional self. However, your physical body cannot be ignored as it is a part of you as well. Stabilizing your energy periodically through energy treatments and anchoring your light in nature is beneficial to both your balance and progress. Furthermore, reminding yourself that you are participating in a monumental shift of change for all of humanity highlights the need for kindness and patience with yourself and others. Many are stepping up and out into their light exploring the new dimensions of themselves and the possibilities that exist. Reach out for assistance from your multi-dimensional guides who are ready with the clarity and wisdom necessary for this journey of riding the tide of energy of an emerging new world.

Wealth

The energy of wealth on your planet is lopsided and out of balance. This energy now originates from either the energy of lack or entitlement. So, like many of the energies on your planet, the wealth energy has been distorted and has evolved into something far away from its purity of truth. The collective consciousness holds this distortion in the many beliefs and thought forms humanity carries. This is yet another area where the collective holds falsehoods that influence your energetic world and cause constant emotional distress. Additionally, this distortion keeps a structure of creation in place where there are specific rules to abide by when seeking your wealth energy. These rules are not in coherence with unity consciousness. The purity of wealth must be once again anchored on to the planet, stripping away the tainted energy that is visible all around you. How is this done? It is done by focusing on bringing forth the dimensional energy of wealth from universal intelligence through your dimensional self. It is a waste of time to imagine how your human form can be the catalyst for such overwhelming change. There are too many barriers to the shift that the collective would have to make. The most efficient way is to be a carrier of the purity of this energy through the many dimensions of yourself. Again, as you walk the ascension path, you are constantly seeding the planet with the potential of something new through your light waves. You are looking forward not backward. The human existence is all about looking at the past and trying to fix what is broken. We say to you to look at the future you are creating with your light and what is pure truth. Eventually you will look back to the past and see that it no longer influences the present. Allow the universe to do the heavy lifting. Focus on stepping into unity consciousness which holds the purity of abundance in all things. Unity consciousness does not hold this distortion or the beliefs of the past. It is a pure slate on which to create from the light of the multi-dimensional self and the energy of the win-win. Let go of looking at others in the energy of comparison instead look at yourself and the vast light you carry to create. Go forth, discover universal truth and anchor it to your planet. Rewrite the script humanity has been following to once again connect to the purity of the energy of wealth and abundance.

Robots

There is much discussion and fear in your world about robotics and artificial intelligence. Modern science has made it possible to tinker with your humanness. Organs can be replaced; metal parts can be added to the body to improve physical function and genetic manipulation is now a reality. The ethics of restoring the body to optimal functioning at all cost is now one of humanity's looming questions. What is important to ponder is the energy field of the human body and the highway of energetic consciousness that it travels. For example, when someone has a knee joint replaced how does that affect the energy circuitry and is the body still energetically communicating in the same way? The answer is it cannot function in the same way, however, this energy circuitry is not given a passing thought as the body is rehabilitated to its new functioning metal part. The focus is on the biological healing not the energetic considerations of lost pathways of light. Our emphasis for awareness of this is two-fold; the importance of upgrading energy pathways after invasive procedures to the body and decreasing the fear of humans turning into robotic seekers of the fountain of youth. Your human body is one big network of cells that work in unison within a given structure. This structure is also a container of sorts for your energy field and consciousness. Your energy field has a structure that is not dissimilar to the body's. Both structures collaborate assisting your physicality to be alive with consciousness and creative energy, in other words without this energy structure you would act much like a robot. Your brain would process with half of its capabilities much like a computer that runs specific programs. Therefore, it is important to think about your wholeness instead of a body with removeable parts. By ignoring the energy aspect of yourself, you truly act and think like a robot. Your thoughts become repetitive programs you run based on the pre-written software of the collective consciousness. The collective consciousness is the true artificial intelligence that is running humanity by the beliefs of separation. Therefore, your fear of technology may be seeded in the awareness that you now live like a robot taking commands from an outdated collective consciousness instead of discovering your own energetic wholeness. This discovery begins by first becoming aware of and familiar with your energy field and the structure of light that is ever present. Secondly, it is imperative to nurture and balance that energy field keeping the connections flowing and open. You need to tend to your energy as you would administer to a broken bone. If a body part needs attention then the energy field that collaborates with it does too. Many cultures on earth were aware of the importance of treating the wholeness of an individual but much of this truth has been replaced by the distortions of the collective. This ancient wisdom has been lost to the race for so-called progress. Progress is not putting the physical body up on a pedestal to be perfected by intervention at the cost of ignoring the intrinsic consciousness of humanity's creative energy. True progressive evolution is awakening to the dimensional self, expanding the creative flow of light and coming into true energetic alignment. It is valuing the conscious energy field as much as the physical body. That is the wellness to strive for; to know your energy needs as well as your human needs. This gets us back to the knee replacement example and the importance of intervention in an energetic sense. The focus is not only on the physical healing and rehabilitation but also on the re-alignment of energy circuits for optimal light flow. Are the pathways of light open and functioning from the knee to the toes or has energetic communication been compromised? How does this new physical joint affect the entire energy field of the body? These are the questions to be answered when asking for assistance from an energy practitioner.

The Push/Pull of the Collective

Humans are accustomed to controlling their world through the lens of struggle which results in a push/pull energy. This energy is vastly different than synchronistic flow and allowing the creative energy of the win-win to bring effortless creations. When aligned with the beliefs of struggle and no pain no gain, avenues for staying in this synchronistic flow are blocked. These beliefs spur the desire for control and effectively reinforce these collective belief patterns of struggle. When embarking on the ascension path, the light may illuminate more potential experiences or opportunities to collaborate with others. One must not assume that all potentials will be realized and anchored to the earth. Even within unity consciousness there is the inevitable detour due to free will/choice. This can be frustrating at times until you become more familiar with how the synchronistic flow works. The energy of potential has a myriad of ways to come forth but it must be awakened and actualized through choice and intent. For example, you may see clearly that someone has the potential to create an experience in their life. This potential may be in line with unity consciousness and serve the whole as well as the individual. However, this potential may not be actualized into the reality due this person's choice points and intent. On the surface it may look like they are choosing this potential experience but unconsciously they have made another decision that stops the synchronistic flow. This decision to align once again to collective belief patterns instead of the easy flow of energy is due to the doubt that lives within. Doubt reinforces the struggle and says no to a generous universal energy of opportunity and ease. These are important points to remember as your perspective on life widens and you view your world from the lens of potential. The ascension path will open you up to infinite possibilities. Some possibilities will be realized; others flow past as unfulfilled. Do not judge these lost potentials as they represent the beauty of the human existence which wields the energy of free choice in order to know their power of creation.

The Reunification of the Ancestors

As you go forward on the ascension path, you will begin to become more aware of those who have left the planet and are residing in another dimension. This dimension that many call the 4th dimension has layer upon layer of dimensions within it. These layers are not a hierarchy as many may believe but a striation of sorts that feeds the light within those beings that reside there. For they are formless, they are their multi-dimensional selves swimming in a sea of energy light. Due to their connection to the earth and its laws, they continue to have to choose the amount of light that feeds them. The shift you must make is to look upon this dimension and its beings as one of light not form. You give them their form. During a commune with this dimension, you may have an impression of them at a certain age or human form or you may experience a particular feeling or physical reaction. Those experiences and impressions are coming from you not them. They are beaming telepathic light that is activating your memory banks to solidify the connection dimensionally. It does not serve them to take on form, it serves them to know their light. In light form, they can easily commune with other light beings that are there to serve their advancement. Now that the earth has ascended, this dimension of beings has been melding into the 3rd dimension a bit more making access to these ancestors seem closer than ever before. There is an eagerness of many of these beings to come back to the earth and participate in human form in the advancement of the human evolutionary state. Others are content to reside in this 4th dimension for eons of time. All of them have a choice to be made. Can they come back to an ascended planet with the old scripts they have written for themselves? More importantly, can they come back with the amount of light they currently carry and still stabilize themselves on planet earth? The answer is no. Their current energy cannot stay balanced on an ascended planet. The ascended earth is a place where the knowing of the multi-dimensional light and the human form walk hand and hand, each knowing themselves completely. In their current state, they know their light but their awareness of it is an either/or situation. They see themselves leaving behind their light to engage in human form.

Starseeds

Help has arrived in the form of a new generation of light potential called starseeds. The earth has called forth assistance in shifting the dimensional energy of humanity. The universe has answered this call by providing light beings from various star systems who have incarnated into human form. They are on a mission to participate in creating the new emerging earth. They are the builders of this new world as they connect to the consciousness of unity while demonstrating how to live this new paradigm. Starseeds are awakening now in greater numbers to remember their part in the ascension process. They, like everyone who comes to planet earth, have been shrouded in the collective consciousness of the 3rd dimensional human existence. However, their light is starting to shine through this shroud of energy and they are remembering their purpose. As the light begins to activate, they become painfully aware of living in a world where beliefs and cultural agreements do not make sense. Starseeds carry ideals based on wholeness, peace and unity. Separation is a foreign concept that is difficult for them. Many of these starseeds will find their voices in protest of the antiquated cultural systems. Others will offer potential solutions to age old problems. This shift is going on now and will last for some time as older generations will continue to demonstrate a resistance to change. In this paradigm shift it is the younger generations that will guide the older ones which is counter to the past. Your world will change dramatically under the influence of these young ones who are on a mission to serve humanity in this evolution of consciousness. Their mission is not an easy one at this time because they are up against the resistance energy that is created from the collective consciousness. They are challenging old beliefs and stimulating new thought forms that are counter to the status quo. This takes a great deal of energy for the obstacles they face at this time are numerous. However, they are suited for their mission and have the resilience to push forward with their ideals. When fully awakened to their mission, they can activate and assimilate the necessary light that the world needs to undergo such rapid change. Each individual starseed has a plan that will unfold as they awaken to their purpose and participate in the ascension process. In the beginning of this awakening, they will need energetic support and community to stabilize and balance their light. They must see themselves as the light they are with the creative abilities to move the world into unity consciousness. At this time, starseeds need to be nurtured and shielded from the judgment of the collective. They carry with them the experiences of true freedom and connection with their light which will lead them to the wholeness they seek.

Energy Practitioners

True healing comes from once again connecting to the purity of your light. This connection to your origin has always been there waiting for your return. Your evolution depends on remembering this connection. Your physical body needs to be reminded of the potential of light it can assimilate through contact with the multi-dimensional self. The body can then become more resilient to an ever-changing world and the dimensional shifts that the earth is undergoing at this time. By choosing the ascension path, you are essentially asking for upgrades in your energy field and a direct connection to the vast reservoir of light that is now available to you. Although it is tempting to try to create a fast track to the light on your ascension journey, you have a physical body that must come along for the ride. Therefore, the mental, emotional and physical bodies must be taken into consideration. One way to assure a faster path forward is to work with an energy practitioner that is attuned to the light-filled fields you carry. Establishing a relationship with an energy practitioner that is accustomed to working with the light and understands the goals of ascension is paramount. Not only are they equipped to keep you in balance, they are also a resource for mental information and emotional support. The ascension path can feel complex at times as humanity has not walked this path before. Surrounding yourself with others that understand how to awaken, activate, and assimilate light can be helpful to your progress. Your abilities and purpose will become more apparent as you connect to your multi-dimensional light. Energy practitioners can provide a safe emotional cocoon where your wisdom can blossom. You deserve this support and nurturance from both your multi-dimensional guides and the human energy practitioners that share your desire to see you actualize your potential.

Adaptation

Your progression on the ascension journey will illuminate the contrast between living in your dimensional light and living as a human being in the collective consciousness. It can become tempting to turn your back on this human side of you, resisting the energies of the collective, as you assimilate more dimensional light. The key to successful bridging and stabilization of your physical body is adaptation using your light. Adaptation does not mean an acceptance of the old antiquated beliefs and systems of the collective consciousness, quite the contrary. The act of adapting is stepping into an observer mode and noticing where you can bring your dimensional light to specific people and situations within the collective. This observer mode places you in a neutral energy where the wholeness of you can be in harmony with your surroundings. This is an important point to remember; the goal of ascension is not to leave the human existence but to discover your dimensional self and experience it through living in a human state. It is not an either-or situation. True energetic bridge building is bringing back the dimensional light so the mental, emotional and physical bodies can express in full wholeness.

Observation

One of the most helpful ways to speed up your ascension progress is to see your world through the eyes of an observer. It then becomes quickly apparent what beliefs and habitual patterns are holding you back. Observing is a neutral state of energy that can easily awaken the truth within you. It can give you the clarity and deep understanding for those situations that are not in accordance with your light. Instead of allowing yourself to repeatedly be triggered into emotional feelings and mental thoughts that do not serve you, reach for a state of pure observation. Much of what triggers your reactions are mere habitual energy patterns. Observing these habits is obviously the first step in stepping into neutral energy. Imagine coming to your world for the first time and observing without judgment the behaviors and actions of humanity. Now focus down on something specific that is in contrast to your own belief patterns. Remember you are pretending that you are not a part of this world only a visitor for a short while. Witness without judgment allowing the energetics of the situation to pour forth. Focus on the energy not the language or the images. Notice how following the energetic patterns guide you to be only an observer in a neutral energy state. You are now looking at the situation from your dimensional light instead of old energy patterns based in the collective consciousness. You are engaging with your world from the purity of you. This results in the clear discernment of how to proceed and create actions based on your own inner truth. Remind yourself often that it is always an option to become the observer before engaging and experiencing an encounter with another person. Practice observation in those situations that attract habitual patterns and old thinking. Detach yourself from the energetics of frustration and judgment by stepping into being the observer of your own world. Allow yourself to feel the peace of being in a neutral state of energy where light is your guide. Observation assists you to live as a human connected to the light and wisdom of the dimensional self.

In Conclusion

Living in your fast-paced world does not always foster the importance of taking the time to fully contemplate whether concepts and information fit with your inner truth and purpose. The act of pondering can enable you to observe your world through the lens of nonjudgment. All words and images carry a vibrational energy that can trigger your emotions and stimulate your mental critique. Any new information or concepts can challenge your mental constructs to either resistance or acceptance. Looking at information as energy is an interesting concept in itself and can be useful in determining what is truth for you. On the ascension path, you will come to realize the importance of looking at life through the energy of light. Light is the energy of creation and it rides the wave of neutrality. There is no need to judge light only to contemplate the wisdom within it. Ask yourself these questions: Can you stand back and look at your world through the eyes of an observer as we do? Can you contemplate new concepts with the intention of being in a state of neutral energy? What information triggered your resistance or expanded your perspective? What, if any, of our observations and concepts can now be accepted as yours? Have you become more aware of how your human existence can be a place of opportunities to expand in your light? Expand into your light by walking your ascension path from a deep place of curiosity and energetic perspective. Question and choose what may be appropriate for you and your purpose both as a human and a multi-dimensional being. You are the expert in knowing how to experience and create from your inner truth. We celebrate you and your quest for the knowledge that will lead you back to the purity of your light. We acknowledge you with great gratitude for your interest in this book. May the energetics of this book speed you on your ascension path. And most importantly, we ask that you see yourself as we see you. To us, you are the infinite light of potential that the universe and planet earth has been waiting for.

Energetic Exercises

The human experience relies on using the 5 senses to actualize the energy of its physical form. Multiple patterns of energy are set into your reality by utilizing and participating with your mental, emotional and physical senses. From your growth as a child to an adult, you practice and exercise the energy that develops into the human you are. Even when some limitation impairs your perception, your resilience and creative ability can seek out new ways to actualize the human experience. These energetic patterns come through the practice of being human. You have learned and mastered the art of becoming a human being. This did not happen overnight. This was something you practiced every minute of your existence. This mastery is now your demonstration that you possess an innate ability to create and put into practice energetic patterns to serve your existence. Additionally, this innate ability also serves your quest for connecting and knowing your multi-dimensional self. Therefore, through the practice of particular patterns of energy, new concepts of unity consciousness can be anchored and realized through the human experience. By exercising your multi-dimensional energy in pertinent ways, you can begin to create and know yourself as the light that you are. With that said, may we suggest you try practicing some of the following energetic exercises. These exercises are designed to help you set forth the building blocks of energy that support unity consciousness and consequently help you know yourself as light. First ponder these exercises and apply them as you feel called to. A particular exercise may be more relevant in your day-to-day experiences than others. Secondly, focus specific attention to any affirmation that is given within the exercise. These affirmations can illuminate any discord between new truth and old collective belief patterns. Remember, words carry a vibration of energy that can speed up or hinder your progress so do not judge the simplicity of the word. Allow your own feelings to surface to assess your alignment with the vibrations of the words. Ask yourself "do I truly believe what I am speaking?" If not, look closely at any beliefs or feelings that have surfaced through the interaction with the words. Finally, challenge yourself to look deeper to examine any energetic obstacles to stating or practicing these truths with integrity. These exercises were created for maximum assimilation of truth and light to assist you in bridging the gap between your human existence and your multi-dimensional self. If you are living simultaneously in both worlds you are practicing and integrating the most suitable vibrations that create the energy patterns of unity consciousness. And in doing so, you will once again be recognizing your own innate ability to create a new reality born of unity consciousness and to master the expression of the multi-dimensional self.

Light Exercise

Every time you focus on the vibration of light through your thoughts or by speaking the word, you chip away at your connection to collective consciousness. The freedom you aspire to, by becoming the sovereign being that you are, is through practicing your awareness of the light. It might seem simple but think of how you have been conditioned by the collective by hearing and repeating the same beliefs and thoughts over and over. Your human conditioning has mental memory loops that cycle repetitively from years of learning to participate in your human world. This sluggish energy presents nothing new and instead reinforces past patterns. Untethering from the collective consciousness starts with simply being present with your thoughts of light energy. This exercise can be done anywhere and takes no special ability. Think light, speak light and feel the light within you. Feed yourself repetitive light-filled thoughts, speak the word "light" often and view the light through images. Ponder "light" while listening to your favorite music. You have the skills to bombard yourself with light and through this assimilation you can condition yourself away from the collective consciousness. New insights and wisdom become available to you and you begin to pulsate with energy that is truly yours not recycled patterns and beliefs. Practice activating and assimilating light through focusing on what is important; yes, it's the light. Allow the light to gently show you the path to the freedom and inner wisdom you seek.

Image Exercise

Another valuable tool for accessing and traveling with your multi-dimensional self is by using a photographic image of a portal of light. Any pleasing image that has a light-filled area that you can interpret as a pathway or gateway to a place full of light will work. There should be a focus point where mentally and emotionally you are drawn in, ignoring the surrounding items around this point of light. Stare at this focal point before you meditate with the intention of waking up to your dimensional self. By doing this you can speed up your connection and activate your light. This concerted effort to see and know your light through the human sense of sight can also help to bridge the gap between your dimensional self and your human existence. It strengthens the communication between your physicality and your energetic light. During your meditation, you may feel more balanced which makes you more receptive to those messages or insights that are waiting to come to you. The natural world is full of examples of light-filled pathways that can stimulate your multi-dimensional light. The vision you possess is not only functional but a gift to facilitate your awareness of the beauty of the human world. Allow this gift to show you the beauty of the light within by providing an opportunity to travel from a light-filled image which advances you on the ascension journey.

Bubble of Light Exercise

See yourself as a bubble of light and hold this image when you are wondering about your multi-dimensional self. It is easy to connect with your physicality as this container of energy has been with you for many lifetimes. Your human presence is spotlighted by the collective consciousness and becomes central to how you operate in your world. We are now challenging you to see yourself in an additional way which is amazingly different from what you are accustomed. It may seem unobtainable at times, like trying to hold on to a mist, but it is just as real as your human existence. Using images to become more familiar with this part of yourself is key. Your dimensional light is all around you and you emit this light without even knowing it. Becoming conscious of this light and working with it for the benefit of yourself and others is the purpose for this awareness. It is time to facilitate and upgrade your existence in this light and bring forth this energy for the emerging new world. When you focus on being a bubble of light or your humanness in a bubble of light, you can begin to imagine playing with this light. Step into a magical child's mind and use this perspective to explore the light of your dimensional self. Expand and contract your light, visualize it moving upward and downward, and as layers upon layers of light. Picture it much like walking into a dream, ethereal and soft, reacting to your every mental and emotional thought form. Now from your intention, use your light to create. Aim the light forward on your path, imagine it projecting outward and see it anchor itself to the earth. The more you work with this light in this way, the reality of your multi-dimensional light will become apparent. And just as you are aware of every finger and toe of your human body, you will have that familiarity with your light-filled self. Practice getting to know the special light that you are through your intention of accepting the dimensional self. Over time you will walk as a bridge between your physicality and your dimensional self. Build this bridge by exercising the bubble of light.

Trail of Light Exercise

Another way to become familiar with your multi-dimensional self, is to imagine you are trailing bubbles of light energy with every physical step you take. Once again use the magical child's mind to imagine your dimensional self as a bubble of light. Connect fully with intention to your light in this way and allow your 5 senses to engage with this light-filled part of yourself. At first you may only use one of your senses to heighten your knowing of your light. Let whatever physical sensations rise to the surface and guide your experience. In this moment in time, see it, feel it, know it and be your light. Now visualize or mentally focus on your large bubble of light casting off smaller bubbles of light.

These small bubbles float off you waiting for your direction. This may give you a lighter physical sensation. Again, with your intention, direct these bubbles to trail after you as you walk forward. Imagine this light energy flowing behind you, anchoring the bubbles of light to the earth and leaving a refreshing clarity of energy. When using the trail of light, there is no need to mentally think about transforming energy in any specific way. You can rest assured that emitting light always serves the earth and its inhabitants. Additionally, when you are searching for a meaningful solution or contribution to a chaotic world, the trail of light is available as your high vibration answer.

A New Meditation Exercise

Now that you are communicating with your dimensional self, a new style of meditation can help accelerate your process. This is an active form of meditation where you visualize or focus on the knowing that you have successive rivers of pulsating energy. These rivers of light expand out from all areas of your energy field and are ready for exploration. This exercise can be combined with a quiet time in a comfortable space for optimal experience. For those who enjoy the outdoors, sitting surrounded by the sounds of nature can give you a unique connection with the new emerging earth. Either way it will assist you in becoming familiar with your light and how best to move within it. This exercise begins by choosing a number between 5-12. Pick the first number that pops into your mind. Now sit comfortably, close your eyes and visualize your solar plexus the gateway to your multi-dimensional self. From this focus point imagine your light expanding upward from your shoulders in a blast of energy. Again, focus on the solar plexus and see the light expand downward to the top of your toes. If you find visualizing this difficult, allow yourself to hold the thought of this and trust that it is happening. Some of you may feel a rush of energy or even a pulsating sound. Know that the way you experience it will be right for you. Imagine the solar plexus expanding into a larger ball of light, that expands in front of you and behind you. The light is picking up speed now moving outward and in a circular motion. Soon this motion defines layers upon layers of light flowing like rivers to their dimensional destination. Breathe deep into this light and allow yourself to travel with the intention that you will flow with the dimensional light that corresponds with the number you have chosen. Trust that this experience will unfold for your greater good. There is nothing to ask, look for or wonder about. Allow yourself to completely feel immersed in the river of light and become familiar with that energetic space. You are always in control of this process and can adjust the speed of which you travel within the dimension. Call on your multi-dimensional guides for any reassurance or assistance you may need. Gently guide yourself back from the experience and center yourself back into your physical body through focusing on your solar plexus. Breathe deep with the knowing you are building a bridge between your multi-dimensional self and human existence.

Leveling Up Exercise

Speak these words: "I am light. I am multi-dimensional light." Close your eyes, repeat this affirmation 3 times while focusing on your solar plexus. Take a deep breath and go within this gateway of light with the intention to relax and enjoy the comfort of your multi-dimensional self. Call forth your multi-dimensional guides and feel the expansion of your energy. There is no purpose or agenda just the sweet communion of light that is you. Rest in the energy as long as possible. Breathe yourself back into your body with long slow breaths. Become aware that you are carrying a higher vibration of energy now. Assimilate this light into your physical body by these words: "I anchor light to every cell of my body releasing the stress of the human world. I am centered and connected in my physical presence."

Siren Exercise

In your world, you have many reminders of fear through the agreed upon sounds from the collective consciousness. The sirens of an ambulance, fire truck or police car can put you on high alert and raise a cautious vibration within your physical body. Mentally, you try to locate the sounds and process whether action is necessary. Those living in urban areas may experience these sounds as normal noises of their environment but do they really become commonplace to your nervous system? Your conditioning through these sounds will always trigger an unconscious energy flow that encourages physical, mental and emotional stress. Transforming these energies is simple by using these sirens as a reminder to communicate with your light. Every time you hear a siren, think about your multi-dimensional self and expand into your inner light. Say to yourself "I am my multi-dimensional light. I am light." Repeat this over and over for as long as you hear the siren sound. Through this intentional thought, you neutralize any stressful vibrations within your physical body and emit more light to your environment. Additionally, you can direct your light to those vehicles and recipients of the distress call. Why not use an everyday occurrence that is designed to signal caution to open up your light field? Turn this agreed upon stress from the collective consciousness into an opportunity for practicing your light and becoming more familiar with your multi-dimensional self. Unity consciousness asks you to answer the siren call by residing in your light.

Neutrality Exercise

You will naturally attract more neutral energy as a result of seeking your multi-dimensional light. In order to hasten this process, especially when experiencing various energetic triggers, you can practice holding a neutral state by the following exercise. Start by recalling a person or situation that triggers unpleasant emotions within your awareness. There is no need to try to intellectualize the dynamics instead feel the strong emotions behind this awareness. Connect now to your multi-dimensional self and hold the intention that you will expand into your light. Once you feel this expansion of light taking the place of these strong emotions, imagine that you are looking through a window at the person or situation. As you peer out the window, affirm to yourself that "I am an observer and my light illuminates the neutrality within. I see the truth of this experience and release the need for habitual patterns from the collective. I observe the truth in all things." Repeat this exercise as often as necessary especially when there are triggers that hold more power over you than others. Eventually, you will be given the gift of clarity over the situation which prompts beneficial actions. You will also experience more understanding and compassion when interacting with others. But most of all, you will begin to intentionally disconnect from the collective consciousness in order to feel the honesty and truth of your own emotions. Consequentially you live and demonstrate the world of unity consciousness.

Observer Exercise

Imagine looking through a window at situations that trigger your emotional frustration and unbalance. Allow yourself to breathe slowly and deliberately while saying the following: "I am an observer and my light illuminates the neutrality within. I see the truth of this experience and release the need for habitual patterns from the collective. I observe the truth in all things." Now focus on any of the words of this affirmation that seem ingenuine to you and ponder them closely. Ask yourself the following questions: How best can I observe without an emotional experience? How can I release need for the constant cycles of emotional energy? What stops me from staying in a neutral energy and creating situations that are aligned with my light? Remind yourself often that the role of the observer is always an option. Observation in a neutral state of energy can promote satisfying experiences with others through breaking the cycle of habitual emotional energy.

Starseed Activation Exercise

If you are a starseed, you need to balance your energy quite frequently in order to work from a place of clarity and your own innate wisdom. The influence of the collective consciousness can drain and fatigue your energies. Refreshing the light matrix with this simple exercise can help you assimilate more active light and renew your resolve. This exercise begins by closing your eyes, placing your hands on your solar plexus and breathing in light. Slowly and deeply breathe in the light and exhale the light five times. Imagine the light building and expanding inside your core. Now focus on the word "Purpose" repeating this word slowly 3 times. Imagine or feel the vibration of this word. Direct this vibration to connect with the light building in the solar plexus. As the energy vibrations join together, the light will expand outward and flow to all light centers. As the light expands, ask for clarity of purpose by saying the following: "I am the light and I am ready and able to actualize this light by my purposeful actions." Continue to expand the light as you ponder this statement. Repeat it frequently until your energy feels renewed and refreshed.

In Conclusion

These energetic exercises can help support your intention to not only communicate with your light but to express that light in your everyday world. Practicing these energetic patterns can call forth the experiences that bring peace, calm and a sense of purpose. The more you engage in light-filled participation with your world, the more you vanquish the doubt that hinders your progress along the road to ascension. Strive for those experiences that validate your own innate ability to master being and actualizing your own light.

Questions & Answers

What is the purpose of ascension?

Humanity must know itself as light in order to evolve further and retain balance while living on a dimensional changing planet. Ascension is humanity's next evolutionary step.

Why should I participate in the ascension process?

The dimensional shift of planet earth is laying the energetic foundation and support for humanity's transformation. Now is the time to walk the planet as both a physical human and an awakened dimensional self. Those that have an interest in this book have carried within them a vast potential of creative energy that can help build a world based on unity consciousness. The time you have been waiting for is here.

Why does the earth have to purge itself from energy?

The earth's new dimensional energy does not resonate with the old 3-dimensional vibration. The collective consciousness has seeded repetitive patterns that are not in alignment with building unity consciousness which is the centerpiece of the new earth.

What are the first steps in taking in more multi-dimensional light?

By reading this book and pondering the concepts, you have awakened your multi-dimensional self and started to activate the light within you. This book is designed to communicate with both your multi-dimensional self and your human thinking mind. Gaining information and understanding is good but receiving light at the same time is even better. The energy of the written word has been telepathically given through a light connection that maintains the integrity of the energy and delivers it for maximum benefit. Each time you ponder a concept or use the energy exercises you are activating and assimilating more of your inner light.

How can I best connect with my multi-dimensional self?

Practice connecting to your light through the solar plexus center. Hold the intention that dimensional light is your focus. Use the language of light tools and explore telepathic communication. Release old concepts and structures of energy that limit you from seeing this part of yourself.

Can I continue to work with my past spiritual guides along with new multi-dimensional guides?

Working with guides is always your choice and their service is seen as a support energy to your own innate wisdom not as a replacement for your own truth. Multi-dimensional guides are best suited for assisting you in exploring your light through the dimensional self. Their primary focus is supporting your ascension journey and not your day-to-day participation in your human existence. Your past guides have focused on developing the consciousness of the human experience. However, they can continue to give you familiar reassurance and validation as you explore a telepathic communication with your new multi-dimensional guides.

Do multi-dimensional guides have names?

Light beings carry a light signature expressed as an energy vibration that you will become familiar with when you communicate through your dimensional self. This energy signature is not easily translated into what you would call a human language name. However, for ease in building a supportive relationship with you, they may adopt a common name from various human languages.

What types of energy characteristics are within each dimension?

This is for your exploration and knowing. Dimensional energy needs to be experienced not categorized.

What other star systems are assisting our ascension process?

There are many collectives of light beings in service to the light from Pleiades, Lyra, Arcturus and Sirius. Many other star systems will make themselves known through telepathic channels when their service is called upon.

Does my ascension journey change how I see my connection to God or Source Energy?

The ascension journey can enhance and broaden your experiences with your connection to God or Source Energy. Your evolution into the greater light that you are changes your perceptions from the viewpoint of limiting human beliefs to one of expansion through the dimensional self. To know the purity of your origin as light is to experience your ultimate connection to all that is. This purity is your birthright and the refinement of what it is to live as a fully realized human.

What is the role of religion in the ascension process?

It is up to you to discover the truth and light within the constructs of religion. The ascension process is knowing yourself as the light that you are, therefore, you can always choose how to express your light from your human existence.

How can I stop participating in judgment?

Judgment is a repetitive pattern of energy that flows continually within the collective consciousness. At this time, your connection to this group consciousness is strong and ever present. Practicing observation and connecting to neutral energy fields can disconnect you from the collective consciousness. Therefore, you have the autonomy to break the cycle of judgment and chose energies best suited to your evolution. You free yourself from judgment as you free yourself from the energy of the collective consciousness by knowing yourself as light.

What will happen to the collective consciousness when we move into unity consciousness?

Humanity will transform from one consciousness to the other through evolutionary phases. The concept of separation and subsequent created belief patterns will be released until only original truths remain. Humanity using their multi-dimensional light will combine this original truth with the light of universal truth to create from the concept of unity.

How will the physical body change as humanity embraces the ascension journey?

In the past, the physical body has been used as a primary platform to experience a greater growth of consciousness and evolution. However, some of this growth has been to the detriment of the longevity and fully functioning capabilities of the body. Due to the separation constructs of the collective consciousness, evolutionary growth has been created through pain and suffering instead of communing with original light. Thus, disease and illness become an accepted and an inevitable consequence of transforming the consciousness in this way. In the future, the ascension process will pave the way for the body to use light from the dimensional self for healing, renewal and the release of limitations. The physical body will no longer become the reservoir of toxic emotional and mental energies.

How do we change from the chakra system to the multi-dimensional system of light?

Over time one system will meld into the other. The ascension process which consists of activating and assimilating more light will pave the way for the new light system to become fully functional. This new system becomes the primary connection to the multi-dimensional light that is necessary for your evolutionary growth.

How will our relationship with the mineral/crystal kingdom change?

The earth's ascension process has helped the mineral/crystal kingdom release and clear past collective consciousness energies. Many of these minerals have been tainted with the energies of exploitation, judgment and greed. However, they are now ready to be seeded and programmed with various vibrations of universal light in order to support the new emerging earth. This may change their core properties of energy that you are familiar with but their replacement energies will be of a higher dimensional vibration. Look to these minerals with fresh eyes, asking how you can be of assistance and allow your dimensional self to connect to their new potential of light.

How will our relationship with animals change?

Many animal species will leave due to the needs of their changing consciousness. Communication with the remaining new earth species will expand and humanity will value their contribution to the whole. Some that have primarily offered their containers for nourishment, will no longer have that purpose. The changing consciousness of the animal kingdom will evolve in partnership with the ascending earth and the closer collaboration with humanity.

How can I best be in service to the earth and humanity?

Embrace you light and expand into your multi-dimensional self by walking the road to ascension. Trust this one truth; you are the light your world needs at this time.

THE ROAD TO ASCENSION

About the Author

During this time of ascension and rapid evolution, Jan Mahloch is telepathically communicating with multi-dimensional light guides who are in service to humanity. Through the use of channeled energy, she is able to provide the concepts, messages and wisdom from universal intelligence. Jan's many years of delivering practical guidance from the angelic realm has also prepared her for these changing times. Her channeled readings are insightful, positive and provide the necessary guidance on how to follow one's ascension path for greater light. For further information about Jan or resources for the ascension journey, please visit her website.

www.triooflight.com

Made in the USA
Las Vegas, NV
10 August 2023

75919656R00103